WAKE UP, KICK ASS, REPEAT

A Guide to Self Perseverance Within
the Military Spouse Life Cycle

DR. KENDRA LOWE

Wake Up, Kick Ass, Repeat:
A Guide to Self-Perseverance in the Military Spouse Life Cycle

Published by

Thrive On, LLC

ISBN: 978-0-578-62142-5
Library of Congress Control Number: 2019920771

Editing by Jen Zelinger, Twin Owls Authors' Services
jenzelinger@gmail.com
Book design by Nick Zelinger, NZGraphics.com

First Edition

Printed in the United States of America

Contents

Acknowledgments

Writing a book is much harder than I thought but also more rewarding than I could have ever imagined. I would first thank my husband, Patrick, for devoting endless hours of dialogue to help create this book, picking up the slack at home, and telling me to "stop talking about it and go write it!" Thank you for always being my biggest fan. To our children, Brianna, Amberlyn, and Gabriel, you are my inspiration to make this military life better.

I'm eternally grateful to my mentor Dr. Kerry Hinkle, who has continually helped forge my path as a psychologist, including countless hours editing this book. His guidance has taught me patience, persistence, and a love for helping others. This would not have been possible without him.

Writing a book that incorporates part of your life is a surreal process. I'm forever indebted to the military spouses who have bravely shared their stories: Beth Autrey, Kendra Gilpatrick, Diane Teschner, Lucy Witzig, Nicole Fike, Hakeem Walton, Claudia Watson, Crystal Cox, Lindsey Rowe, Linda Ambard, Marybeth Lowe, and those who wish to remain anonymous. And to CMSgt Nathan Cox, a true warrior. Thank you all.

To my editing team! Dr. Kerry Hinkle, Molly Bennett, Marybeth Lowe, Robert Lowe, Kate Spickert, Nick Zelinger, and Jen Zelinger, it is true what they say—a book is only as good as your team, and you all are exceptional!

To my family: my mom, Sharman Toomey, an incredibly strong person who always tells me "I can do anything I set my mind to," my dad, Robert S. Marks, whose service to our nation instilled my unwavering patriotism, and to all my extended family who have supported our military family through years of separation and sacrifice. You all are the foundation of who I am.

Finally, to all of those who have played a significant part in getting me there: Col. Britt and Meredith Hurst, Joyce Graham, Cathy Amrhein, Evie King, CMSgt Kris Rogers, Dr. Ingrid Herrera, Brittany Boccher, Kristen Christy, and Corie Weathers. Your support and encouragement helped make this vision a reality.

Introduction

There are no great men, only great challenges that
ordinary men are forced by circumstances to meet.
—Sully Sullenberger, *Making a Difference*

One hundred twenty-three. In seconds, it's really not that much. In days deployed, it bears a little more weight. In lives, that number just became more significant. On September 26, 2019, the Department of Defense released, for the first time ever, the number of military spouse suicides. In 2017, that number was 123.

Each number represents one of our own—a military spouse who couldn't find a way out, a life gone too soon. It's very hard to talk about. However, we must talk about it because one of those spouses could have been the energetic friend you met for morning walks with your children strapped into your jogging strollers. It could have been the new spouse you met at a Friday squadron social who told you they were struggling to find a job in the area. It could have been the "seasoned" military spouse you have always looked up to who "has it all together." Could it even have been you?

This book is a resounding call to stop and "ReSet" the way we think about military spousal stress. It is intended to challenge how we think about the unique stressors military families face and to reflect upon the experiences of those who have gone through similar circumstances. More importantly, through this ReSet, military spouses will gain tangible tools aimed at helping them cope with the unique challenges of military life.

Brené Brown eloquently writes in her book *The Gift of Imperfection*, "Our stories are not meant for everyone—hearing them is a privilege." Time and time again, I have been humbled and honored by the brave spouses who have shared their stories with me and, ultimately, with you. Whether you work through this guide individually or as a group, cherish the personal stories, take time to reflect on your own experiences, and open the door to new possibilities.

We cannot accept another year with the loss of 123 military spouses.

We Are Strong—We Are Vulnerable—
We Are Capable—We Are Military Spouses

1

Setting the Stage
Finding Your "Kick Ass"

There can be no rainbow without a cloud and a storm.
—Larry Wall and Kathleen Storm

My Experience

We all have specific dates that are permanently penned as part of our story. They cannot be erased, edited, or revised. They are published as a written reminder of life-altering events. June 29, 2015, is one of those dates for me. It is the day my husband, three small children, and I were abruptly delivered to a foreign country and landed on the Patriot Express runway of Kadena Air Base, Japan—a place where I was immediately hit by suffocating humidity, what I later referred to as "Florida on steroids" because there is nothing normal about having to wipe down your interior walls when they visibly sweat in the summer. Physically struggling to breathe only amplified my mental anguish about leaving friends and family behind halfway around the world. My family endured the thirty-six-hour flight with military families who faced identical futures: a military assignment overseas. The grueling journey became a permanent chapter in my story, one that will not change but, nonetheless, shaped the stories yet to come.

At seven p.m. (1900 hours), we disembarked the plane and walked to the large Rescue Squadron sign proudly displaying a guardian angel.

While this kind gesture was extremely thoughtful, I remember thinking all I wanted to do was get out of my sweaty clothes and crawl into bed. We left the terminal on Kadena Air Base and were transported by car to our new base housing. I opened the door to our new home and right away noticed the dated interior complete with dropped ceilings, fluorescent lights, and concrete beige walls. Taking it all in, I tried to hide my disappointment. I reminded myself I could do anything for two years but, at the same time, wished there was a secret time machine that could transport me through the next two years with minimal damage.

I walked into the galley kitchen and took a deep breath. My husband's new boss and his wife had been part of the welcome party, and at this point, she approached and questioned me, "Well, what do you think about your new home for the next four years?"

Four years! I did not know our assignment was going to be four years. I was under the impression this was only going to be a two-year assignment. I was devastated. I gripped the table next to me and prayed my weakened legs would hold me up.

I no longer had the strength to hold it together. My face instantly distorted to reflect a mixture of exhaustion, disappointment, sadness, and anger. My husband picked up on it across the living room and, assuming it was pure fatigue, politely asked everyone to go so we could settle the kids into bed. He later admitted that night that he, too, had just learned that we would be staying for four years. And just like that, it was done.

Initially, I struggled with the prospect of being overseas for four years with three children under the age of five without the support of family and friends. During that time, I also had a difficult time shaking my sadness. To make things worse, my husband started work immediately and went on several temporary duty assignments (TDYs) while

I settled the kids into kindergarten and a local pre-K program two days a week. As a means of self-preservation, I forced myself back into healthy habits by working out and getting involved in the local community. However, for some reason, I didn't bounce back as quickly as on previous TDYs, and for me, that was unusual. By the end of December, my husband had grown tired of my melancholy attitude. Recognizing his concern, I came to the realization that something had to change.

I made up my mind that I did not want to feel displaced any longer or to feel sad throughout our entire four-year assignment. In an effort to revitalize myself, I stayed up late one night putting together a journal of personal reflections. In the process, I noticed a flood of emails into our inbox for after Christmas sales. (In Japan, the junk email comes late at night.) Possibly out of avoidance, OK, definitely out of avoidance, I opened an advertisement for Wallwords. Subconsciously, I was drawn to this advertisement because I knew my husband would not support painting the base housing walls, and this was my only option to personalize the décor. The website featured intricate designs to stick on your walls, and I ended up stumbling into the section that had phrases and quotes. Among these were quaint messages to express love, kindness, and gratitude. None of these seemed appropriate for my current state of mind—except one. There it was, in large black letters: *Wake up. Kick Ass. Repeat.* I knew I had to have it. I immediately ordered the phrase in the largest font available and expressed shipped it to our overseas PO box. Ten days later, I proudly displayed the saying in our dining room. It became a daily mantra—a sometimes hourly reminder—of what I knew I was capable of and how I was going to get through the day.

The mantra remained on our wall the entire four years we were in Okinawa; sometimes I even forgot it was there until I would hear one of my daughter's friends whisper and giggle, "Your mom has ASS on your wall," or a new neighbor would stop by, pause mid-sentence during introductions, and snicker at the wall. "It's my daily motivational tool," I would explain. But as time went on, it began to serve an even greater purpose. On March 5, two months after I had adhered the placard to our wall, my mother called to inform me my grandmother had passed away. (I would end up losing all three remaining grandparents in our first three years on the island.) During my time at Kadena Air Base, I navigated through exceptional highs (defending my doctoral dissertation, our children excelling in school, and my husband's successful command tour), fear of loss (my husband and his squadron's rescue in 2016 of five crew members on an MV-22B Osprey that crashed into shallow water off Okinawa, and in 2018, the Tham Luang Thailand cave rescue of twelve boys and their coach, in which the entire world joined us), and several lows (unemployment, underemployment, injured children, prolonged single parenting duties, and distance from familial support systems). As a consequence, "Wake up, Kick Ass, Repeat" became my personal mantra for coping with the perpetual challenges of being a military spouse.

The path I walked as a cadet at the Air Force Academy as an active duty service member, and now as a military spouse, has given me a front-row seat to many of the traumas, setbacks, successes, discriminations, and celebrations that military families experience. The common bond of military life and its unique challenges have resulted in what Sheryl Sandberg, author of *Option B*, has coined as a "collective resilience,"[1] a way of life that allows a military spouse to come to grips with the adversities they face and keep moving forward. The more military spouses I met, the more I noticed a cycle of acceptance, ReSetting, and perseverance that this unique lifestyle calls upon a military spouse to manage. Military spouses must navigate personal sacrifices with grit, determination, and humility, while at the same time solo parenting, living in a foreign country, and reestablishing life in a new location—or sometimes all three! While all military spouses have a shared sense of hope, experiences, and commitment to family and country, the nature of the military lifestyle makes each one of our paths look different. Every one of us walks a unique path. Given the many challenges faced by military families, it seems perfectly normal for military members and their families to accept that it is OK NOT TO BE OK!

The stories I witnessed and personally experienced, even sometimes endured, would lead you to believe that military spouses and their families would readily raise their hands seeking help and support. However, this is certainly not the case! A tacit disconnect exists between observable external stress levels of military spouses and the more accurate, but less observable, internal levels of stress. In other words, what's going on outside does not always match what's going on inside. This disconnect is concerning because of the number of military spouses who not only suffer significant stress but do so alone. It was this disconnect that fueled my ten years of research aimed at better understanding military spouse stress and about how bad the stress really is, as well as the unique contributing factors of military lifestyle.

In 2008, I began researching the source and stress levels among fifty Air Force spouses in Valdosta, Georgia. Specifically, my research focused on the impact of the active duty member's time away from home, whether it was due to deployments, training/education, or the temporary duty of a military family.[2] My initial findings were disconcerting. At that point, I was given the opportunity to expand my research in 2013 to North Carolina (compliments of the US Air Force). At that time, I broadened my research to include several military branches (Air Force, Army, and Navy) and interviewed more than 200 spouses.[3] Although I walked the path daily, I was shocked when my original findings were confirmed. At that point, I knew I needed to learn more about spousal stress in hope of developing tools to help this unique group navigate these challenges. Through my research, I developed a desire to validate and bring awareness to the unique nature of military spousal stress.

With the help of a few instrumental mentors, the major findings of my research gained broader attention. Most significant were the findings that 27 percent of military spouses report significantly high levels of stress, while 20 percent have a higher, clinically significant, level of stress.[2] In other words, approximately one in four military spouses wake up every day under a heavy layer of stress that builds day by day, week by week, and year by year. Unfortunately, many military spouses perceive this stress as normal, unaware of how dangerously close they are to clinically significant levels of emotional, social, or physical distress. Beth, an Air Force spouse, beautifully illustrates this misconception.

Spinning Plates
Beth's Story

I think that we, as military spouses, are unaware that we often operate at an elevated level of stress—it's a fact we sometimes forget. I sometimes visualize stress in my own life like I am spinning plates; I can keep them going until you add another plate, and then it all falls apart. Military spouses operate at that level much of the time. I know that I have some of the same concerns as everyone in the world; I worry about family, money, and health. But on top of that is this uncertainty about where I am going to live next, when I will move, if my husband will deploy, if he is going to be gone TDY, how long will he be gone, and when he will be back. The addition of these unique stressors is important for us to acknowledge. I think we tend to tell ourselves, "I've got this. I've done this before. I can do it again." After nineteen years of military life and countless moves, every change is STILL stressful. Even after all this time, things still get to me, and at such times, it is important to remember that it's OK to ask for help. As a member of a military family, we need to acknowledge that we are at this higher level of stress and that it is OK to ask for help. At such times, it is OK to ask a spouse or friend for help, and yes, in some cases, you may need to ask for professional help. It's OK. We need to remind ourselves that there are resources specifically built to deal with the stressors associated with military life.

—Beth Autrey, Air Force Spouse

Fortunately, military spouses are starting to understand that their stress is real, significant, does not discriminate based on demographics, and may extend throughout a military career. During a speaking engagement on military spouse stress at a Pacific Air Forces (PACAF) Command Team briefing, I had an encounter with a veteran military spouse. This woman in the audience caught my attention after she asked several questions. After the presentation, I had the opportunity to continue the conversation with her, and she admitted to battling stress throughout her twenty years in the Air Force. Later, when our paths crossed again, she shared how the presentation changed her perspective about being a military spouse. Kendra Gilpatrick tells her story.

Helping You Helped Me
Kendra's Story

The first time I heard the statistics about military spouse stress, honestly, I was surprised by the magnitude of the stress and how it didn't matter how old you are or what rank the active duty member is. It really challenged my point of view and caused me to evaluate my behavior. Since hearing about military spouse stress and the impact it has on so many people, I've been more attentive, more compassionate, and more forgiving, particularly with myself. I am more willing to talk about the stress I feel. I now give myself latitude to take breaks and to take care of myself so that I can take better care of others. I also found that by acknowledging the stress, I became more relatable and approachable. I was very thankful for the information. Now I'm more involved in helping alleviate some of that stress for others, and in the process, it alleviates some of mine.

—Kendra Gilpatrick, Air Force Spouse

While Kendra's personal illustration of stress is an important first step in understanding the lives of military spouses, we can all agree more needs to be done to address the long-term challenges unique to military life. The goal should not be to just overcome occasional isolated incidents of stress but to recognize and address the unique challenges faced by ALL members of military families. We not only need to share information with incoming families about some of the different experiences they will have—but also provide the knowledge and skills they will need to successfully navigate such challenges. Because of the unique characteristics surrounding this type of stress, additional services and specific levels of care need to be available to military families.

As a first step in addressing this need, the military has acknowledged the importance of resiliency. Indeed, anyone who has been in the military for even a few months has learned the definition of "resilience" or "a person's ability to bounce back after a jarring setback." Because this is looked at from the military side rather than the family side, military resilience training consists of specific programs aimed at helping military personnel develop the mental, physical, social, spiritual, and behavioral strength necessary to endure military life and assist their families through the same process.

The military has focused on resiliency, and although this is an attainable goal, it should be understood that it is characteristic of some of the most successful individuals today. Take, for example, the well-known inspirational story of one of our own, Kristen Christy, 2018 Armed Forces Insurance (AFI) Branch Spouse of the Year. In 1983, just before her sixteenth birthday, she suffered a massive stroke that paralyzed her right side, forcing her to learn how to walk again when doctors told her it was impossible. Tragically, twenty-five years later, her first husband committed suicide after returning from a deployment, leaving her to raise their two sons alone. In 2015, just seven years later, her son went missing after being diagnosed with bipolar disorder and has yet to be found. Fast-forward to today, she is now traveling the world sharing her message that we are "all survivors of something" and championing a proposal for March 4 to be commemorated as National Survivor's Day. Her remarkable resilience is well deserved and inspiring, yet it can seem wildly unattainable for many who are experiencing the weight of ordinary, everyday stressors.

While resiliency may be easy to define, it is much more difficult to achieve. Indeed, many of the challenges faced by military families are intense and of long duration. And while the military spouses face unique challenges over extended periods of time, and are often praised for being resilient and strong, there is a disconnect between social and personal resiliency. This disconnect can place extremely high expectations, and often increased pressure, on individuals merely trying to survive. The fact is that we may not always feel resilient, but this external expectation prevents us from owning up to the truth. One example could be seen in my own family while we were stationed at Fort Bragg, North Carolina.

My Experience

In April 2010, my husband and I moved from Valdosta, Georgia, to Fort Bragg, North Carolina. While I enjoyed supporting the unique Special Operations mission my husband had selflessly chosen to serve, the mission took my husband away from home for extended periods of time. I definitely felt the stress of being responsible for setting up a home and support system while he was deployed and on TDYs. My emotions vacillated between feeling the joy at witnessing our daughter's first steps and apprehension over my husband's repeated absences, due to high-operational tempo.

During our first year in North Carolina, there were several formal and informal events within the unit. Some my husband and I attended together, but to many, due to his deployments, I went alone. During one particular promotional event, a senior officer recounted the highlights of an officer's career by culminating his speech with genuine praise for the promotee's supportive wife. This respected spouse was well cherished within the military community for her countless volunteer hours planning successful events for military spouses. The speaker looked directly at the wife and, with warm sincerity, firmly stated she truly was the "epitome of a Spartan wife." (I would later learn that this is a very common reference used to describe military spouses in Special Operations). The audience shook their heads up and down, nodding in approval, but it struck a personal nerve. Reacting to the association between military spouses and Spartan women, I became concerned that the military spouses were, therefore, expected to be by definition "disciplined, powerful, and threatening."[4]

I knew at that time that I was different from the woman he praised. At the time, I had little discipline in my life and seemingly lacked control of almost everything. I did not feel powerful. I wasn't even sure I was capable of tackling the daily demands of military life without my husband. Yes, I knew military spouses were absolutely capable of Spartan performance and that we all embody and interpret Spartan capabilities in different ways with what we are required to endure and overcome. However, at that moment, I didn't feel deserving of being called a Spartan wife next to this amazing group of spouses. I recall trying to disappear for fear that someone would discover I was an imposter. I worried I might have to ask someone for help, yet I wanted to be a worthy Spartan wife. I feared that day would never come.

A universal space needs to be constructed for spouses to feel comfortable to say they are not OK. Military spouses will be better prepared when they are allowed to recover and take a deep breath before learning and implementing coping skills. As I looked back over my own experiences and heard the stories of others, I saw that there is a distinct cycle of specific stages of life as a military family. Once an understanding of the cycles and emotional/behavioral responses that come from each cycle is in place, it is easier to thrive despite challenges. As noted below, I drew upon my recent experiences while immersed in Japanese culture to create this, what I have come to refer to as "the fundamental military spouse life cycle."

My Experience

While living in Okinawa, Japan, for four years, I had the opportunity to immerse myself in Japanese culture. While initially dreading the assignment, I knew that after four years I would miss the local cuisine, Eisa drummers playing outside Gate Number Two in the summer, my children playing freely as if still in the 1950s, the overall respectful nature of the culture, and the symbolism that was woven into their daily lives. I was intrigued when my husband's unit presented him with a Japanese sword, a **Katana**, at his farewell BBQ.

Squadron members and their families stood on the beach and attentively listened to the senior enlisted leader as he detailed an analogy of the samurai sword to leadership. He astutely described the process of how the Katana was made by highly skilled swordsmiths, first selecting the raw material, typically steel called "tamahagane," to serve as the center of the sword. Next, using forged heat, the Japanese swordsmith would strengthen the sword and create a long, sharp edge. In the final stage of polishing, the skilled craftsman would spend weeks honing the sword with special grinding stones often passed down through multiple generations. The long and tenuous process was done with great pride and respect. As such, it was critical for swordsmiths to take time to restore the prized sword after long periods of wear and use in battle or blunt-force trauma. Like the swordsmith to the Katana sword, the vital role of a military leader is to continually refurbish his weapon (squadron) in this same cyclical fashion so that it remained ready if called into battle again.

I was captivated by the analogy, and I couldn't help but think how the relationship of the Katana sword and swordsmith also mimicked the lives of military spouses and our well-being. Each of us is made of a raw material, or our current well-being, that needs to be understood based upon our unique needs (as individuals and as military spouses). We must be deliberate and dedicate time to restoration after the setbacks we encounter as part of military life. This restoration promotes pride and ownership in our well-being. We can systematically strengthen our well-being through specific techniques that have been proven to help. We should celebrate times in which we persevere as well as times in which we thrive. It is important that we appreciate the cyclical nature of life in order to prolong our own social-emotional well-being.

Adaptation is an important, if not critical, stage in a military family's life. The very nature of the day-to-day life of a military family means that a military spouse will be forced to confront and cope frequently with the many challenges this lifestyle brings. However, teaching military families effective ways to cope is much more cost-effective and empowering than letting time and experience teach families how to adapt to this life of service. When Lisa Bradley and Cameron Cruse built their multimillion-dollar business, R. Riveter, selling handbags made by military spouses, they successfully showed how forward thinking impacts a military spouse's life. Success stories like these highlight the fact that this world is full of possibilities despite the unique challenges of military life. Ultimately, we must embrace the unique nature of military life by ReSetting the way we think, as described by the following Army spouse.

Rickety Rollercoaster

I feel like I am on this endless, rickety rollercoaster. I deliberately chug up the tracks to the top, and I sit there waiting for the fall— because I know it is coming. I just don't know when it is going to be, where it is going to be, and what it is going to be yet. Then it hits; my husband gets tasked with a 365-day tour in Afghanistan. I plummet to the bottom with that sickening feeling in my stomach, afraid that I won't be caught at the bottom—afraid that the bottom is too vast and too deep. But I find the bottom, and I am raw. Military spouses reach out to help, but there is nothing to do to help because the fact is you can't change the situation. So I climb inside myself and wait for it to get better. Sometimes it takes weeks or months, and I lose a little of myself each time. But I know I'm capable of being happy again because I've been there before, at the top of the ride. It just gets harder as time goes on to chug up the tracks, and I can't help but think there must be a better way for me to do this."

—Anonymous, Army Spouse

Military Spouse Life Cycle ReSeT

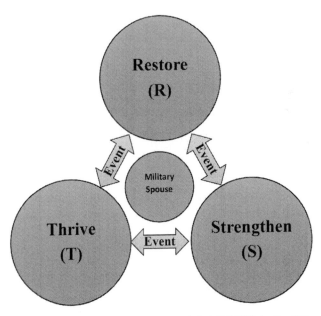

Figure 1. Lowe, K. 2019. *Military Spouse Life Cycle ReSeT*. Thrive On, LLC.

Military spouses are exceptionally unique. Everyone has had a varying degree of stress, challenges, setbacks, successes, and failures. However, the uniqueness of military life and responsibilities give spouses a unique experience. These experiences form the center, like the raw material of a sword, of who we are and who we will become in the future.

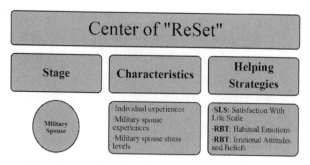

Center of "ReSet"		
Stage	**Characteristics**	**Helping Strategies**
Military Spouse	·Individual experiences ·Military spouse experiences ·Military spouse stress levels	·**SLS**: Satisfaction With Life Scale ·**RBT**: Habitual Emotions ·**RBT**: Irrational Attitudes and Beliefs

Table 1. Lowe, K. 2019. "The Center of the Military Spouse Life Cycle."
Thrive On, LLC.

Restoration (R) is a critical stage for military spouses. The focus of the restoration stage is to regain stability, or the point at which one begins to design their unique sword, before tackling upcoming challenges. This is where a spouse learns to adapt to a unique set of social and emotional expectations. Arriving at this stage is different for everyone. It could be a prolonged period of stress from an assignment, a last-minute deployment, a TDY, or struggles with employment due to location. Spouses must pause, ReSet, and take time so that they are prepared for what lies ahead. However, with the constant expectation to "have it all together," combined with unavoidable stress and the current tempo of our forces, most military spouses do not fully grasp the significance of the restoration stage. Unable to fully recover and feeling the social pressure to be swiftly resilient, many military spouses experience severe social and emotional stress. Such stress is often exhibited by prolonged periods of anxiety and depression.

The Strengthening (S) stage gives the military spouse an opportunity to sharpen his or her skills. Japanese swordsmiths use forged heat to give the sword strength and a sharp edge.

The acute skills gained by the spouse during their strengthening stage will give them the ability to absorb setbacks, implement adjustments, and move forward. These skills will provide you with the opportunity to ReSet after disappointing setbacks. Ultimately, the goal is for military spouses to be able to reinforce each other and create a form of collective strength.

The final life cycle stage is where a spouse embraces a moment of personal success: **Thriving (T)**! This can manifest itself in several ways: meeting a career goal, seeing the world of opportunity through your child's eyes, and/or a personal level of healthy emotions are just a few examples. The last stage of the creation of a Japanese sword is one in which the craftsmen take great pride. It involves the polishing and final finish, which is long and often tedious, due to the continual grinding of the blade to a fine tip. The sharpness of the sword and the ability to keep the edge is dependent on both the angle of the edge and the material used in the process. Just like the crafting of a Japanese sword, a military spouse's ability to thrive is based on their ability to successfully move through each stage of social and emotional development.

Without a doubt, stressful **Events (E)**, or setbacks, are part of a military spouse's daily life. A sword can grow dull over time from constant use and pressure—or it can experience a complete break upon impact from a single catastrophic blow. To a spouse, these setbacks are what cause them to dull and break. Setbacks can cause social-emotional isolation from friends and family members who support our daily lives. Becoming aware of our personal life cycle, knowing ourselves, and maintaining awareness provides the psychological and social support needed by military families.

The life cycle of a military spouse requires us to persevere in spite of setbacks. Perseverance is defined as the ability to "continue the course of action even in the face of difficulty or with little or no indication of success."[5] Just as the Japanese craftsman must hone the sword, the military spouse must hone their ability to persevere, whether it's through a PCS, deployment, comforting children left behind, securing *another* job, or stretching a tight budget—the list is different for everyone. We do this to serve the needs of our nation and the expectations of our military community and to support the ones we love. As noted in the Air Force Rescue creed: "These things we do—that others may live" is just one of the many constant reminders military members and their families see daily. Perseverance is a necessity to survive within the military.

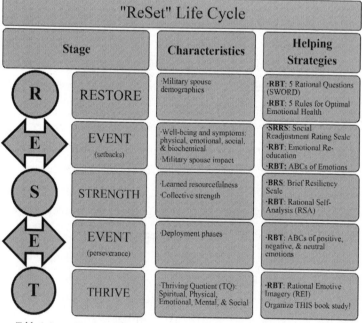

"ReSet" Life Cycle

	Stage	Characteristics	Helping Strategies
R	RESTORE	·Military spouse demographics	·RBT: 5 Rational Questions (SWORD) ·RBT: 5 Rules for Optimal Emotional Health
E	EVENT (setbacks)	·Well-being and symptoms: physical, emotional, social, & biochemical ·Military spouse impact	·SRRS: Social Readjustment Rating Scale ·RBT: Emotional Re-education ·RBT: ABCs of Emotions
S	STRENGTH	·Learned resourcefulness ·Collective strength	·BRS: Brief Resiliency Scale ·RBT: Rational Self-Analysis (RSA)
E	EVENT (perseverance)	·Deployment phases	·RBT: ABCs of positive, negative, & neutral emotions
T	THRIVE	·Thriving Quotient (TQ): Spiritual, Physical, Emotional, Mental, & Social	·RBT: Rational Emotive Imagery (REI) Organize THIS book study!

Table 2. Lowe, K. 2019. "Characteristics and Strategies of ReSet." Thrive On, LLC.

The extent of our personal experiences and/or setbacks are NOT the greatest predictor of whether we thrive or not as military spouses. Rather, it is our ability to restore our social-emotional/spiritual energy coupled with our ability to persevere that makes thriving as a military spouse an achievable outcome. Despite the often unpredictable and uncontrollable circumstances of military life, it is important for a military spouse to acknowledge that they are in control of their social-emotional reactions. This control can be achieved through Rational Self Counseling (RSC) or Rational Behavioral Therapy (RBT)

Rational Behavioral Therapy

Rational Behavioral Therapy (RBT), developed by Dr. Maxie C. Maultsby, is comprehensive self-help, as well as a method of psychotherapy that encourages people to take a rational view of the world. RBT specifically deals with three types of learned human behavior: cognition, emotions, and physical actions with four specific goals.[6]

Rational Behavioral Technique 1

COPE: The Four Specific Goals of RBT

C	• Cope successfully with future living
O	• Overcome stressful situations quickly and safely
P	• Prevent future problems in daily living
E	• Establish self-help tools for long-term results

Figure 2. Lowe, K. 2019. *COPE*. Thrive On, LLC. Adapted from Maultsby, M.C. (1990). *You and Your Emotions*. Self-Help Books Division: Kentucky.

RBT has been proven to be a practical and effective way to treat common emotional and behavioral concerns. RBT tools and techniques serve as the theoretical premise upon which this book is written, by gradually building concepts within each stage to help military spouses COPE.

Isolation
Renee's Story

I get frustrated with myself because I know I am capable and smart, and I hate that I struggle to function. It's maddening. I know there are ways that I can feel better and deal with situations better, but I just don't know where to begin. One of my closest friends (another military spouse) invited me to a resiliency weekend over a year ago, and I just couldn't bring myself to go. Reflecting back, I should have gone because it was advertised as a weekend built specifically for military spouses with motivational speakers, childcare, and even free time. It sounded perfect but for one thing: I had to actually sign up. I had to get out of my house. You see, I had isolated myself for so long that the fear of going and sharing myself with a large group of strangers that would not be there for me in the future was just too much for me to overcome.

—Renee, Marine Spouse

We need to build a strong barrier to combat military spouse stress, which is an undeniably constant and persistent force in our lives. I used to think, prior to years of research, that the robust resiliency trainings mentioned were the ONLY solution to military spouse stress. I know now that they are

NOT. Military spouse stress has not decreased. In fact, suicidal concerns have continued to increase.[7] These trainings are a step in the right direction but alone are not effective enough to reduce the amount of stress that is so desperately needed. Renee's anecdote perfectly illustrates the current gap in assistance for our military spouses. Military spouses desire the intimacy of being alone or with a small group of known and trusted peers combined with a continued access to support. This individual approach enables spouses to work through the unique challenges associated with military life while giving them self-help tools to foster perseverance and the ability to thrive. Search any military community, and you will find various book clubs alive and well for this very reason. I know as a military spouse that it is imperative to create an enduring, intimate, safe space for military spouses to restore, strengthen, and thrive—to ReSet the way we think about life within the military.

This book is designed to be read individually or with a small group of peers. Each chapter introduces specific characteristics that address the military life cycle and self-change through the use of RBT self-help tools.[6]

This is for you, Renee, and the thousands like you, so you have the tools necessary to build lasting support in the comfort of your home or with close friends without giving up your peace, safety, and security.

Reflection Questions

(1) Without reading ahead, what stage do you think you currently are in the military spouse life cycle? (Restoration, Strengthen, Thrive)

_____

_____

_____

_____

_____

(2) Why do you think you are currently in this stage?

_____

_____

_____

_____

(3) How long have you been in this stage?

_____

_____

_____

_____

(4) Have you attended resiliency training in the past? If yes, what were your thoughts? If not, reflect on why you have not attended.

_____

_____

_____

_____

_____

(5) Have you heard of Rational Behavioral Therapy? Write down your reaction to the four goals of RBT presented in the chapter.

_____

_____

_____

_____

_____

(6) What is your current level of happiness? (Take the assessment on the next page.)

_____

_____

_____

_____

_____

Exercise
Assess Your Current Happiness

For a quick tool to assess your current level of happiness, work through the questions below.

Fordyce Emotions Questionnaire[8]

In general, how happy or unhappy do you usually feel? Check the ONE statement below that best describes your average happiness.

_____10. Extremely happy (feeling ecstatic, joyous, fantastic)

_____ 9. Very happy (feeling really good, elated)

_____ 8. Pretty happy (spirits high, feeling good)

_____ 7. Mildly happy (feeling fairly good and somewhat cheerful)

_____ 6. Slightly happy (just a bit above normal)

_____ 5. Neutral (not particularly happy or unhappy)

_____ 4. Slightly unhappy (just a bit below neutral)

_____ 3. Mildly unhappy (just a bit low)

_____ 2. Pretty unhappy (somewhat "blue," spirits down)

_____ 1. Very unhappy (depressed, spirits very low)

_____ 0. Extremely unhappy (utterly depressed, completely down)

What percentage of the time do you feel happy, unhappy, or neutral? (Write down your percentages to add up to 100 percent on the following page.)

On average:

The percent of the time I feel happy: _____ percent
The percent of the time I feel unhappy: _____ percent
The percent of the time I feel neutral: _____ percent

The average score for happiness (out of 10) is 6.92 from a sample size of 3,050 Americans. The average score for percentages are as follows:

54.13 percent happy
20.44 percent unhappy, and
25.43 percent neutral.[9]

Sources

1. Sandberg, Sheryl, and Adam Grant. 2017. *Option B*. Milano: HarperCollins.

2. Lowe, Kendra N., Katharine S. Adams, Blaine L. Browne, and Kerry T. Hinkle. 2012. "Impact of Military Deployment on Family Relationships." *Journal of Family Studies*, 18 (1): 17–27. https://doi.org/10.5172/jfs.2012.18.1.17.

3. Lowe, K. 2016. "5 Ways to Manage Military Spouse Stress." *Military Spouse Magazine*, 12 (8).

4. writer873. 2019. "The Women of Sparta: Athletic, Educated, and Outspoken Radicals of the Greek World." *Ancient History Encyclopedia*. https://www.ancient.eu/article/123/the-women-of-sparta-athletic-educated-and-outspoke/.

5. Duckworth, Angela. 2016. *Grit: The Power of Passion and Perseverance*. Toronto, Ontario: HarperCollins.

6. Maultsby, Maxie C. Jr., and Allie Hendricks. 1974. *You and Your Emotions*. Lexington, KY: Psychiatry Outpatient Clinic, University of Kentucky Medical Center.

7. Sonethavilay, H., Maury, R.V., Jurwitz, J. L., Uveges, R.L., Akin, J. L., Coster, J. L., and Strong, J.D. 2018. "2018 Military Family Lifestyle Survey: Findings and Analysis." Washington D.C.: Blue Star Families Department of Research and Policy.

8. Fordyce, Michael W. 1988. "A Review of Research on the Happiness Measures: A Sixty Second Index of Happiness and Mental Health." SpringerLink. Kluwer Academic Publishers.

9. Seligman, M. E. 2002. Authentic Happiness: *Using the New Positive Psychology to Realize Your Potential for Lasting Fulfillment.* New York: The Free Press.

2

Setbacks
Embracing the Suck

*Love yourself, accept yourself, forgive yourself, and be
good to yourself because without you the rest of us are
without a source of many wonderful things.*
—Leo F. Buscaglia

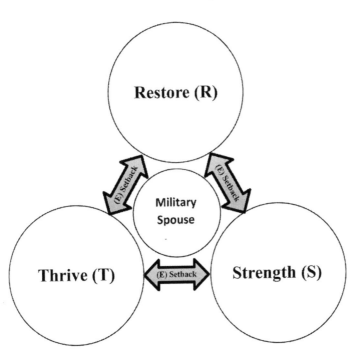

Setbacks Defined

As a child, when my mom gave me a choice to hear the good news or the bad news first, I picked the bad news every time. It quickened the blow of the bad and made the good that much sweeter. Let's start with the hard stuff we face as military spouses, so we can appreciate the good that is yet to come.

By definition, setbacks are things that cause a delay or even stop our progress. Naturally, we do not like them. Setbacks force us to take notice of the stress in our lives. Military spouses certainly have their share of stress—large and small, joyful and tragic. These events can be challenging, causing all kinds of setbacks. The goal of this book is to encourage you to take those necessary steps forward to address the setbacks and emotional snares we all fall prey to and to give you tools to move successfully through the various stages of the military spouse life cycle.

My Experience

On August 6, 2011, ten days after my second daughter was born, a US Ch-47 D military helicopter with the call sign Extortion 17 was shot down, killing all thirty-eight people on board. It was the greatest single-incident loss of American lives in Operation Enduring Freedom—Afghanistan. Three of those Special Operations airmen were assigned to my husband's unit. It shook our community to its core, a true emotional blunt-force trauma.

When it was time for the memorial service, I squeezed my round, post-pregnancy body into a black dress and prepared my eighteen-month-old daughter and ten-day-old daughter for the trip to Ft. Bragg for the official ceremony. I felt numb. It had never hit this close to home.

We entered the large hanger packed with standing room only. An American flag was hung that spanned the entire width of the stage. For me, the memorial service was one of the most emotional events in my life. But assuredly, nothing compared to the spouses and families who lost their husbands, sons, fathers, and brothers. On our drive home after the ceremony, my husband turned to me and informed me he had to deploy to Afghanistan, to the same location, to support the same mission. I was devastated, but I could manage nothing more than, "OK," as I tried to accept this unexpected deployment.

As we stood in our bedroom and held our farewell embrace, I vividly remember thinking, for the first time ever, "He might not come home." I could barely breathe. Without words, we knew this goodbye was markedly different. I told him with very little confidence that I would survive. His response, "I don't want you to just survive this; I want you to CRUSH this." Days later, he deployed.

A week later, I took our dog, Lexy, into the vet for her scheduled ACL reconstruction, necessitated by a freak accident at a local dog park. (Who knew dog parks could be dangerous?) We had originally scheduled her surgery before we knew of my husband's deployment, and I considered rescheduling it but knew it could not wait the five months until he returned. Life must continue, even though this was one more thing to add to my already full plate.

After a successful surgery, we brought our dog home and made her comfortable in our master bathroom with her awkward white cone of shame. I tucked in my toddler, nursed my new baby, and climbed into bed. Around midnight, I woke up to the sounds of crying. Assuming it was my infant girl, I went to pick her up and soon realized it was not the sounds of an infant at all, but rather a whimpering dog. I trudged down the narrow hall and peered over the wooden baby gate into the master bathroom. There was blood everywhere. I blinked my eyes several times, hoping I was still in a dreamlike state, yet the blood remained. Our dog had somehow managed to remove the staples from her left leg, and the gaping wound was bleeding everywhere. I climbed over the gate, found a bandage in our linen closet, and wrapped her leg. I surveyed the bathroom and started cleaning. Then I heard it, this time definitely infant cries, and knew it was time to feed my baby. I climbed over the baby gate again, changed out of my bloodstained pajamas, and fed her. At that point, the dog whimpered louder. And then I heard new crying sounds. All the noise woke up my oldest, and then she was in the master bedroom, crying with outstretched arms, wanting to be held. I clearly remember thinking that I was positively NOT crushing this deployment; I was barely surviving. In fact, I was closer to an emotional breaking point from the relentless setbacks.

Early the next morning, I loaded the girls into the car to head to the veterinary clinic. When we arrived, I unbuckled my three-week-old daughter, walked into the building, and like any good mother, handed her to the receptionist. My oldest followed closely behind me, and I told her to sit on the black leather couch. I went back outside to the car and gathered Lexy into my arms and carried her into the reception area while we waited to see the veterinarian. When we were called back into the examination room, the doctor took one look at my crew, and his face affirmed what I thought: we were a train wreck. He assessed Lexy's leg and gently told me that he needed to keep her at the clinic to care for her. I reluctantly let go of her red leash and carried the girls back to the car. I cried all the way home. I felt I had failed to meet our dog's basic needs.

The clinic called daily to provide reports on how Lexy was improving, and yet, I kept telling myself how much I had failed her. After ten days, she was ready to be released, and we were all eager to pick her up. I collected her favorite stuffed duck, and we drove to the clinic. When the doctor emerged from the back with Lexy, he asked if it was OK to remove her plastic cone, as they had formed a bond; I agreed. I graciously thanked him for his tender care of Lexy and then asked about where to settle the bill. My husband and I had discussed that the ten-day stay would be expensive but knew it was in the best interest of all of us. The doctor paused, looked at me, and said, "Your husband is deployed, right?"

"Yes," I replied.

"This one is on us; it is the least we can do for a family that is serving our nation."

My words caught in my throat, and my eyes started to burn. I finally uttered, "Thank you," and gave him a hug. I left the clinic for the second time in two weeks, barely able to navigate the car through tears, and found myself driving into town to the nearest Panera Bread. I purchased and delivered lunch to the entire staff. However, this small gesture in no way compared to the emotional strength I gained when this team helped pull me out of a spiraling situation. As I reflect, I wonder what would have happened if this team did not step up to help or—if I chose not to accept it. I fear I would have continued to struggle, alone, with devastating results, as I was not equipped to help myself. The internal tape playing in my head kept telling me to "survive," not "thrive."

Stress vs. Distress

Setbacks inevitably lead to stress because it forces us to go in a direction we were not expecting, and this can be upsetting. The most common example for military spouses is having a permanent change of station (PCS). By nature, a PCS causes the entire family to stop, change directions, and start again (and again and again). One of my favorite descriptions of the PCS cycle looks something like the figure below.

The Military Spouse PCS Cycle of Emotions

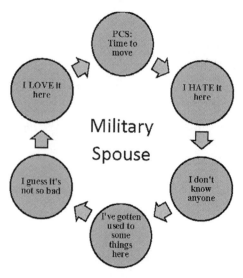

Figure 3. Lowe, K. 2019. *Military Spouse PCS Emotions.* Thrive On, LLC.

As you can see, the stress of moving can cause a series of emotions. Stress then becomes any uncomfortable emotional experience accompanied by predictable biochemical, physiological, and behavioral changes.[1]

"Mere thoughts can set hearts racing and hormones surging."[2] For example, when the stress hormone cortisol is released into the bloodstream, learning and memory, the immune system, bone density, and weight gain, as well as depression and mental illness can all be impacted.[3] In the above example, thinking, "I hate it here," after a move could cause faster heart rates, feelings of sadness, and temptations to self-medicate. However, stress is not a one size fits all. It impacts us all in different ways. What follows are a number of signs of stress.[4]

Signs of Stress

Physical	Faster heartbeat, dry mouth, increased sweating, increased urination
Emotional	Irritable, fatigued, sad, apprehensive, laugh nervously, urges to cry, scream or hide, argues more than usual
Cognitive	Difficulty concentrating, difficulty making decisions
Behavioral	Acting impulsively, prone toward accidents, feel tempted to smoke, drink or medicate yourself
Biochemical	Fainting, increased secretion of stomach acids, decreased immune system, increased cortisol levels, increased blood pressure

Table 3. Adapted from Echterling, C., Staton, V., McKeel, P., and Stewart (2002).
Thriving: A Manual for Students in Helping Professions.
New York: Houghton Mifflin Company.

After looking over the symptoms above, highlight/circle the ones you are feeling right now, today. If you highlighted several of these symptoms, then there is a strong possibility you are experiencing social-emotional distress.

So, what is distress? Distress is when you begin to feel overwhelmed by events or circumstances. The Social Readjustment Rating Scale (SRRS), developed by Dr. Thomas Holmes and Dr. Richard Rahe (1967), measures major life events and their impact. Look over each event, marking down the point value of each event that has happened to you during the last twelve months. After reviewing and recording each of the forty-three stressful life events, sum up the point value associated with each event.[5]

Social Readjustment Rating Scale

Life Event	Mean Value
1. Death of Your Spouse	100
2. Divorce	73
3. Marital Separation	65
4. Detention in Jail or Another Institution	63
5. Death of a Close Family Member	63
6. Major Personal Injury or Illness	53
7. Marriage	50
8. Being Fired from Work	47
9. Marital Reconciliation with a Mate	45
10. Retirement from Work	45
11. A Major Change in the Health or Behavior of a Family Member	44
12. Pregnancy	40
13. Sexual Difficulties	39
14. Gaining a New Family Member	39
15. Major Business Readjustment	39
16. Major Financial Change	38
17. Death of a Close Friend	37
18. Change to a Different Line Of Work	36
19. A Major Change in the Number of Arguments with Your Spouse	35
20. Taking on a Mortgage	31
21. Foreclosure on a Mortgage or Loan	30
22. A Major Change in Responsibilities at Work	29

Life Event	Mean Value
23. A Son or Daughter Leaving Home	29
24. In-Law Troubles	29
25. Outstanding Personal Achievement(s)	28
26. Spouse Beginning or Ceasing Work Outside the Home	26
27. Beginning or Ceasing Formal School	26
28. A Major Change in Living Condition	25
29. Revision of Personal Habits	24
30. Trouble with the Boss	23
31. A Major Change in Working Hours or Conditions	20
32. Changes in Residence	20
33. Changing to a New School	20
34. A Major Change in Usual Types and/or Amounts of Recreation	19
35. Major Changes in Church Activities	19
36. Major Changes in Social Activities	18
37. Taking on a Loan	17
38. A Major Change in Sleeping Habits	16
39. Major Changes in the Number of Family Get Togethers	15
40. A Major Change in Eating Habits	15
41. Vacation	13
42. Major Holidays	12
43. Minor Violations of the Law	11

Figure 4. Social Readjustment Rating Scale (SRRS). Thomas Holmes and Richard Rahe, The Social Adjustment Rating Scale, 1967 in the *Journal of Psychosomatic Research*, 11, 213–218.

** If your summative score is less than 150, you are experiencing a relatively low amount of life changes, suggesting a low chance of a stress-induced health event.

** If your summative score is between 150–299, there is a 50 percent chance you may suffer from a major health event in the next two years.

** If your summative score is 300 or higher, there is an 80 percent chance of developing a stress-related illness.[5]

Are you experiencing symptoms of **stress** ("Table 3")? Is your **distress** score low, medium, or high? It is important to be aware of your levels of stress and distress because if left unattended, our bodies can, and will, begin to break down, as suggested by the first personal story in this book. Such stories will be highlighted throughout the book to help you understand the concepts being presented and what those concepts look like in the lives of our fellow military spouses.

Take the Next Step
Diane's Story

Life is hard—sometimes all we can hope to do is take the next step and hope for the best. I learned this as a military wife, coming face to face with the reality that the next step is sometimes—oftentimes—forced upon us, regardless of our level of preparation. The normal stresses of raising a family, coupled with the unexpected, life-changing inflection points, are already tough.

As a military family, these are compounded by constant disruptions in the form of multiple overseas moves, regular deployments to combat zones, and constant job changes. In "normal" life, these disruptions are considered among the most stressful life-changing events that can happen to a family. In a military family, these are considered the norm. Before you know it, you are constantly functioning at extreme levels of stress—and you're part of a network of people who are all doing the same. And while non-military friends and relatives might see what you're doing as "extraordinary," it is really just you coping with the tough reality of life—you are no different from any other spouse/ mom/friend; those who see amazing things in what you're doing would step up and do it as well were the roles reversed. Knowing this, I once read that depression, anxiety, and panic attacks are not signs of weakness but rather are signs of trying to remain strong for far too long. We have an obligation as military spouses to address these stressors through proper support and coping skills. The story I'll share is one about getting sick and having a baby while overseas, one that added additional disruptions to our already-disruption-filled life. I'm honored to share it and lend my support to this noble cause.

Five years ago, while stationed in Stuttgart, Germany, my husband was diagnosed with colorectal cancer. He was forty-one years old at the time and had been recently deemed fit and ready to return to the fighter cockpit he loved. His diagnosis was a shock to both of us, especially as I was six months pregnant at the time. Within days, Rob faced a very difficult colon resection surgery that would hospitalize him for two weeks. In addition, he was given an ileostomy that required a second surgery to reverse a few months after the first, leading to two further weeks of hospitalization. Grandmas flew out to take care of our three children, ages eight, five, and two. Each day, I took the morning train downtown to be with my husband, returning home after spending a full day with him, only to console our frightened children and to try to decrease the ever-increasing stress to preserve my pregnancy.

Rob's surgeries were extremely tough, and I know being with him, even to sit in silence while he suffered, was a huge blessing for us both because I was able to REALLY understand what he experienced. This allowed me to support him best. When he returned home, the healing was only just beginning; Rob would continue to suffer every day, spending hours in the bathroom— becoming a slave to his body as a result of the absence of his lower colon. It was exceedingly difficult for him and for us, especially as we were not fully briefed on how difficult his post-operative life would be. During the beginning of this lengthy (and still ongoing) recovery, I went into preterm labor at thirty-four weeks.

I would go on to spend four weeks in a German hospital taking care of my premature child. Because we were overseas, my support was limited, and I felt extremely isolated. I wasn't sure I had the mental strength to remain at the hospital with my baby once he was released from the NICU. I was hormonal, unprepared, alone—and I missed my other children who, in turn, missed me. Fortunately, Rob and I deepened our ability to communicate through this experience, and we learned to respect each other's differences in handling our challenges. He needed silence, and I needed people. When I returned home with our baby, Rob was trapped in the bathroom more than I was breastfeeding.

The normal husband stepping in to make dinner when the newborn needed to be fed was not there; Rob was undependable because of his postoperative body. I learned to accept his occasional presence and participation in family life as a gift to be enjoyed—and not an expectation that wasn't met. I remembered regularly holding my breath around five p.m. because I knew I still had to find a way to get through the next three hours. In retrospect, that was probably anxiety, but I didn't even have time to consider that possibility.

For his part, Rob couldn't be trusted to be alone with the children because he couldn't guarantee he wouldn't suddenly have to race to the bathroom where he would be trapped, sometimes for hours. When Rob talks about these times, he always explains that I was, in effect, a single parent. I would agree to some extent, but I would also offer that I benefitted from his mental strength and words of encouragement.

Later, I would learn that for the first six months he was in excruciating pain every time he went to the bathroom. I didn't know this at the time and, even today, I am still so amazed at what he endured. I also know that I would have been severely depressed if I had to endure countless hours every day in a bathroom in pain. I always felt I had it easier, but he knew that his recovery was tough for me and appreciated the support. We had very different struggles during this chapter, but the beauty was that we respected, supported, loved, and found humor throughout it all. I say all of this because it's important to understand that yes, I had it easier, BUT that didn't dismiss the gravity/stress of the situation it put on my own emotions at the time. We as caretakers have to take care of ourselves.

How did I survive? The answer is simple—I had four tools I relied on:

1. *Faith: Rob and I share a very strong faith. We weren't always perfect, and we've both messed up a lot, but we never doubted God's plans, and we never pushed back against what was happening. During this difficult time, we threw ourselves into prayer and trusted in Our Lord. My personal goal was to not be bitter, to not lose hope, and to trust there was a bigger picture. At times, I had clenched fists, but I held true to it, and Rob and I held each other accountable to it.*

2. *A solid team: My husband and children were solid as rock, and I had a purpose/reason to keep going. How we dealt with our challenges directly affected our children. Rob had a fighter pilot mentality, and I leaned into him instead of resenting him. We relied on each other's strengths, and that was beautiful. It wasn't always easy and always fun, but we were a team.*

3. *Other military spouses: My military spouse network didn't always fully understand the post-operative journey, but they always listened, loved, and welcomed me broken. They stood strong while I was weak and never doubted or worried. They were military wives who'd had their own struggles. They hugged me, picked me up, brushed me off, and encouraged me to keep going. I did.*

4. *Outdoor physical activity: Germany has beautiful biking paths, and the kids and I took advantage of those—bike rides served as my mental medicine that first year. We would charge down an incredibly steep and dangerous hill daily; I needed excitement in the midst of the "Groundhog Day" effect and found it through riding bikes on challenging terrain. I think the children needed it too.*

All of this said, there's one final part I've had to come to peace with, one that didn't really hit me until five-plus years after the first cancer surgery. That is, I've lived in constant state of subconscious fear—fear that came out of nowhere with the original diagnosis and, frankly, is there every time Rob goes in for another checkup. I've tried to be on the other side of it. I've always felt like the rabbit climbing under the fence trying to get to the other side—a silly visual I know but one that is very real to me. I can reflect and see that I've lived my life building a plan for Rob's untimely demise—it's driven what schools the children are in, my decision to pursue a career in relationship marketing, and a bunch of other things. Every time Rob coughs, I've envisioned it as manifestation of the return of his disease. I remember him saying, "Every time you look at me, it's like I have cancer again."

Rob is never one to not stand up for what was right, and he was spot on—I was afraid. I tried to control my fear instead of accepting that we never know what our journey will be and to really trust God's plans—easier said than done. I don't think we know what we are capable of until we are pushed a little out of our comfort zone. But when it's too much, we need to give ourselves grace and seek help in whatever form that needs to be.

In my opinion, mental health should be part of an annual physical. I say this partly because you don't know what you don't know, especially when it comes to mental health. More importantly, I say this because by the time you truly get sick, it can sometimes take MONTHS to be seen by a doctor. Whatever your story is or stress you are facing as a military spouse, you may be doing just fine and maybe not. And please take the step to check your mental health so that you are ready for the step you didn't expect.

—Diane Teschner, Air Force Spouse

As suggested by Diane's story, there is a significant need for military spouses to have access to professionals who are not only trained to provide effective interventions but who also understand the unique stress associated with military life. In 2014, the Air Force developed the Comprehensive Airman Fitness Program (CAF). The goal of this program is to "develop Airmen and families who are prepared mentally, physically, socially, and spiritually to carry out their missions." The CAF includes a master reliance trainer (MRT) to help provide resiliency training for military members and families.[6] Also, a comprehensive study by RAND in 2015 further highlights the Air Force's focus on increasing access to mental health professionals with programs like the Military Family Life Consultants (MFLC). MFLCs are licensed professionals who provide free, nonmedical, short-term counseling to airmen and their families without required documentation.[7]

Although some units and installations provide clinicians to support military spouses, unfortunately, such services are not available across all military bases and units. When available, these programs provide valuable training and resources to help alleviate military spouse stress because our stress is SIGNIFICANT.

Military vs. Civilian Spouse Stress

The majority of people learn to handle stress in their daily lives without developing significant social-emotional problems. However, approximately 10 percent of the population cannot handle normal, everyday stress. At any given time, **one in ten** in the CIVILIAN population experiences clinical levels of stress, but how does that compare to military spouses?[8]

Military spouses experience significant levels of stress, as reflected in the Military Lifestyle Survey conducted in February 2014. More than 6,200 military families responded to the Military Family Lifestyle Survey and found 39 percent of military spouses indicated elevated levels of stress, with 8 percent expressing specific suicidal ideation.[9] This study also suggested that military spouses reported a higher level of depression symptoms than did their active-duty counterparts. The Military Family Lifestyle Survey is conducted annually. In 2018, the number of respondents increased to 10,192 military spouses, with suicide ideation increasing from 8 percent (2014) of military spouses to 9 percent (2018).[10]

I feel as though everyone wants to understand military service member suicide but no one cares about spouses back home while their husband is deployed or the impact deployments have on children. No one researches the mental health of families, only the service member.[9]

Military spouses clearly suffer from unique stressors and, in order to assess how military spouse stress compares to their civilian counterparts, the following stress-related exercise was designed.

In the space below, write the names of twenty people you know who have a spouse in the military. Next, put an asterisk (*) next to those military spouses you believe have elevated levels of stress.

1._____ 2._____

3._____ 4._____

5._____ 6._____

7._____ 8._____

9._____ 10._____

11._____ 12._____

13._____ 14._____

15._____ 16._____

17._____ 18._____

19._____ 20._____

Write the number of individuals with **an asterisk** (*) here: _____.

Now calculate the percentage by taking the number with stars and dividing it by twenty.

Write the percentage here _____.

Drawing upon my ratings of more than 200 military spouses, my data suggests that at any given time, 27 percent of military spouses report significantly high levels of stress.[11] Furthermore, of this group, 20 percent have a higher, more clinically significant, level of stress. In short, my research suggests that at any given point in time, a substantial portion of military spouses exhibit <u>measurable signs</u> of moderate to clinically significant levels of stress.[11] In other words, approximately **one in four** military spouses wake up every day under a heavy layer of stress that builds day by day, week by week, and year by year.

How close was the percentage you calculated? Was it higher or lower? Why do you think you got the results you did? Did your population look like the one below?

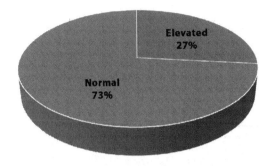

Figure 5. Lowe, K. 2019. "Military Spouse Stress Levels." Thrive On, LLC.

If the available data is correct, the stress level among military spouses is potentially **twice** that of the civilian population. Such findings indicate that military spouses are currently functioning at high levels of stress. Remarkably, research suggests that military spouses experience levels of stress similar to those of single parents.[12]

These findings suggest that the military spouse may experience extended periods of considerable stress. Consequently, military spouses may exhibit behavioral and emotional symptoms suggestive of elevated levels of stress that may require social and/or emotional support. This is a tremendous concern, as I indicated in my article "5 Ways to Manage Military Spouse Stress."

Unsuspectingly, many military spouses perceive such stress as *normal*, unaware of how dangerously close they are to clinically significant levels of emotional, social, or physical distress.[11]

While stress is recognized as a regular part of a military member's life, the amount and impact it has on our overall well-being is not as recognized.

Available data suggest that military spouses may need additional clinical support but that trained clinicians are not always available. Consequently, self-help, as well as peer support, can be instrumental in addressing the unique social-emotional needs of military families.

Rational Behavioral Technique 2
You and Your Emotions

Our life is what our thoughts make it.
—Marcus Aurelius

Emotional Reeducation: Five Stages

The daily life of a military spouse can be extremely stressful. Although we may lack control over the stressful situations, we can certainly control how we respond both emotionally and behaviorally. The goal of this book is to achieve emotional change through Emotional Reeducation. Emotional Reeducation is a concept developed by Dr. Maxie C. Maultbsy (1980) and involves five specific stages:[13]

Emotional Reeducation Stages

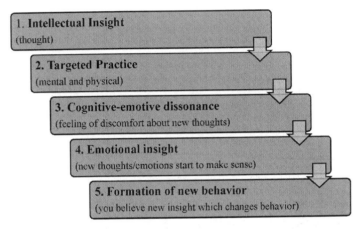

Figure 6. Adapted from Maultsby, M.C. (1990). *You and Your Emotions.*
Self-Help Books Division: Kentucky.

Let's start with **(1) intellectual insight** by understanding the underlying premise of Rational Behavior Therapy (RBT), which is the ABCs of Emotions.

A Rational View of Emotions[14]

The ABCs of how you create your emotions deals with how they are experienced and how you can change how you feel and behave by making specific changes to your thinking.[13] When you have an emotion, you first perceive (i.e., see, hear, or physically feel) something. Next, you think and believe something about your perceptions. Finally, you have a gut feeling caused by your thoughts. To break this down a little more simply, whatever you believe about what you perceive causes you to feel and act the way you do. In Rational Behavioral

Therapy (RBT), this is referred to as the ABC Theory of Emotions.[14]

ABC Theory of Emotions

Figure 7. Adapted from Maultsby, M.C. (1990). *You and Your Emotions.* Self-Help Books Division: Kentucky.

Let's apply this to my experience at the beginning of the chapter.

A. Perception: my husband left on an unexpected deployment, and I saw/heard my dog's pain from ACL surgery.

B. Thoughts: I thought and believed, "One more thing I HAVE to take care of without the support of my husband or family."

C. Emotions: My thoughts made me feel angry and anxious and led me to my actions (crying multiple times throughout this deployment and isolation from friends and family).

Thinking I "HAD" to do one more thing without support made me feel alone and overwhelmed. At the time, I did not have the self-help tools I needed nor a willingness to reach out for help. Fortunately, I had people who stepped in to help, but the honest reality was I was ill-equipped, at the time, to help myself.

RBT is effective because it teaches us to help ourselves by understanding our emotions—more specifically:

(1) how you make yourself feel the way you feel and

(2) how you can change your emotions to make yourself feel differently without having to change the situation.

Many of the Rational Behavior Therapy (RBT) concepts referenced throughout this book may seem like common sense, but with focused study, people grasp the importance of these simple yet significant insights into our emotions. By slowly building on the concepts presented, you will gain the self-help tools needed to handle stressful situations while maintaining greater emotional control.

Reflection Questions

(1) What was your reaction to reading the two stories about social-emotional setbacks?

_____

_____

_____

_____

_____

_____

(2) Describe your most current social-emotional setback. (Remember: a social-emotional setback can be anything that delays or stops your progress.) Briefly describe below.

_____

_____

_____

_____

_____

_____

(3) What symptoms did you experience as a result of the stressful experience? Fill in below. (Refer to "Table 3: Signs of Stress" for a reminder of possible symptoms.)

Well-Being Category	YOUR Symptoms
Physical	
Emotional	
Cognitive (Mental)	
Behavioral	
Biochemical	

(4) Discuss the percentages you calculated. Was your percentage of spouses suffering from significant levels of stress higher or lower than 20 percent? Why do you believe you obtained that percentage?

_____

_____

_____

_____

_____

_____

Exercise

(1) Read the Five Stages of Emotional Reeducation below and write down what you think it means.

   (1) Intellectual insight (thought)
   (2) Targeted practice (mental and physical)
   (3) Cognitive-emotive dissonance (feelings of discomfort about new thoughts)
   (4) Emotional insight (new thoughts/emotions start to make sense)
   (5) Formation of new behavior (you believe the new insight, which your changes behavior)[14]

_____

_____

_____

_____

_____

_____

(2) Read the ABCs of Emotions, and note what assumptions you DISAGREE with.

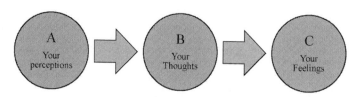

_____

_____

_____

_____

_____

_____

(3) Read through the ABCs of Emotions, and note what assumptions you AGREE with.

_____

_____

_____

_____

_____

(4) Take the Social Readjustment Rating Scale (SRRS). Write your score below. If you are doing this guide with a group of friends, share your score and talk about it. If you are on your own, write down a few thoughts. Having a reference to go back and look at is always helpful!

SCORE:_____

(5) Did you think your score was accurate? Why or why not?

_____

_____

_____

_____

_____

_____

_____

Sources

1. Jr., William C. Shiel. 2018. "Medical Definition of Stress." *MedicineNet*. https://www.medicinenet.com/script/main/art.asp?articlekey=20104.

2. Schwartz, Jeffrey, and Sharon Begley. 2013. *The Mind and the Brain: Neuroplasticity and the Power of Mental Force*. Kbh.: Nota.

3. Bergland, Christopher. 2013. "Cortisol: Why the 'Stress Hormone' Is Public Enemy No. 1." *Psychology Today*. Sussex Publishers.

4. Echterling, Cowan, Evans, Staton, Viere, McKee, Presbury, and Stewart. 2002. *Thriving: A Manual for Students in the Helping Professions*. New York: Houghton Mifflin Company.

5. Holmes, T. H. and Rahe, R. H. 1967. "The Social Adjustment Rating Scale." *Journal of Psychosomatic Research*.

6. Air Force Instruction (AFI). 2014. *Comprehensive Airman Fitness (CAF)*. By Order of the Secretary of the Air Force.

7. Meadows, S., Miller, L., and Robson, S. 2015. "Promoting Resilience in the Air Force." *Airman and Family Resilience: Lessons from the Scientific Literature.* 43–50. Retrieved from http://www.jstor.org/stable/10.7249/j.ctt19rmdbt.13.

8. Burns, S. L. 1990. *How to Survive Unbearable Stress.* Atlanta: International Medical Press.

9. Bradbard, D., Maury, R., Kimball, M., Wright, J., LoRe, C., Levingston, K., Shiffer, C., Simon-Boyd, G., Taylor, J., and White, A. 2014. "2014 Military Family Lifestyle Survey: Findings and Analysis." Washington D.C.: Blue Star Families Department of Research and Policy.

10. Sonethavilay, H., Maury, R.V., Jurwitz, J. L., Uveges, R.L., Akin, J. L., Coster, J. L., and Strong, J.D. 2018. *"2018 Military Family Lifestyle Survey: Findings and Analysis."* Washington D.C.: Blue Star Families Department of Research and Policy.

11. Lowe, K. 2016. "5 Ways to Manage Military Spouse Stress." *Military Spouse Magazine.*

12. Osofsky, J. D. and Chartrand, M.M. 2013. "Military Children from Birth to Five Years." *Future of Children.*

13. Maultsby, M.C. 1990. *Rational Behavioral Therapy.* Rational Self-Help Aids: Wisconsin.

14. Maultsby, Maxie C. Jr., and Allie Hendricks. 1974. *You and Your Emotions.* Lexington, KY: Psychiatry Outpatient Clinic, University of Kentucky Medical Center.

3

Perseverance
Make Your Setback a Comeback

I have not failed. I've only found 10,000 ways that won't work.
—Thomas A. Edison

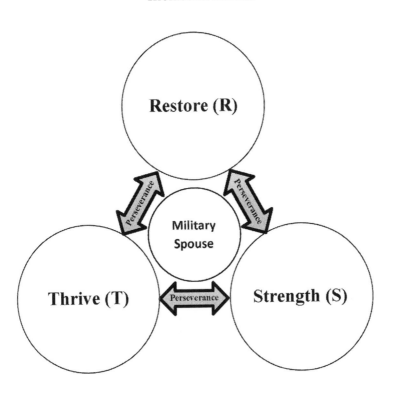

Perseverance Defined

Our setbacks should not and cannot define us. In fact, the life cycle of a military spouse requires perseverance despite setbacks. Perseverance, the second example of an event within the military spouse life cycle, is how we move forward despite the challenges in front of us.

Perseverance is the ability to continue the course of action even in the face of difficult situations or with little or no indication of success. Crafting the strongest versions of ourselves, much like crafting a Japanese sword, is a long and tedious process. Perseverance creates the hope that our continued efforts will be successful. A military spouse must demonstrate perseverance repeatedly. Picking up and moving again, preparing for yet another deployment or TDY, and comforting children, parents, friends, and sometimes even pets left behind are all part of dealing with personal stress. Perseverance becomes necessary to not only survive but to THRIVE! However, perseverance is not always inherently easy. Fortunately, there are specific techniques that can help promote perseverance. While using these skills to maneuver throughout your life cycle will not ease most challenges, they will allow you to continue moving forward despite such challenges.

My Experience

"US military evacuates embassy staff from Yemen over a terrorist threat, Americans are urged to leave." (Fox News 2013)

I wasn't allowed to tell anyone my husband was there, at the embassy in Yemen. In fact, the only person who knew he was there was my brother-in-law, a USAF HH-60 pilot at the time.

I had decided that summer to pack up our dog and thr
travel north from North Carolina to Illinois to spend time with I
friends. As far as everyone knew, my husband was deployed again to
an unknown location. They accepted this as normal and rarely asked
questions, knowing such questions only created more anxiety for me.

I woke up early on August 6 and shuffled down my mom's spiral
wooden staircase to get a cup of coffee. The baby was only two and a
half months old and was still waking up several times a night, so I was
looking forward to a warm cup of caffeine. My mom, a lifelong early
riser, was already in the kitchen, beautifully dressed with makeup on
and ready to conquer the day. I, on the other hand, looked like I had
just stepped out of a bar fight with my shirt inside out, unbrushed hair,
and dark circles under my eyes. I nodded a quick hello that cautioned
it was too early for conversation. I slowly poured a cup of coffee and
walked into the adjacent living room, where Fox News was broadcasting.

"We don't want another Benghazi, so twenty-one embassies have
been ordered to evacuate."

I bit my lower lip. Given the nature of my husband's job, I knew he
would have to stay; he would be the last out, so others may live. I listened
to the rest of the report and tried not to react in front of my mom
for three reasons: (1) I was instructed not to share his location, (2)
confiding in her would not absolve my worry but only add to her own,
(3) and it would only confirm my mother's desire for us to stay longer,
and I could only handle so much "togetherness."

My mom and I had planned to take my two girls to Downtown
Chicago to the American Girl doll store. I wanted to cancel, stay home,
and listen to updates on the news, but I forced myself to follow through
with our planned activity. I knew how much everyone was looking forward to this trip and would feel selfish if I canceled.

We arrived at the American Girl doll store about midafternoon. While the girls stood in the store deliberating which set of matching pink pajamas they wanted, my phone rang. I stepped out of the store briefly to take the call.

"Kendra, it's Matt. I know he's there, and he is safe right now. He won't be able to contact you because he has gone underground. I want you to know we will get him out. He won't be left behind."

My whole body shook; I could barely breathe. And it was there in a flash—the recurrent worst-case scenario image in my head of a blue, official car waiting outside my house. I would see it sitting there, knowing what the military officials were waiting to tell me. I would drive by them, pull into my garage, unload the kids, and hide. They would knock, and I would brace myself for a blow that I knew I would never recover from.

I physically shook my head to remove the image from my mind. I somehow found my voice and thanked my brother-in-law for the phone call. I told myself that I trusted our Special Operators. I knew they would do anything within their capabilities to get our Americans safely out of Yemen. I squared my shoulders and walked back into the store. Really, that was the only rational choice I had, that or crumble, which I refused to do.

Sheer grit and determination got me through that summer and fall. I had just started my doctoral program, and my newly defined goal, coupled with an introduction of new therapeutic techniques, provided tangible tools throughout my husband's long deployment to Yemen. I felt something shift that summer as I started to make conscious choices to be emotionally healthy for myself and for my children. I wanted them to have memories of a healthy, happy mom. However, I think my family and friends felt just the opposite about my decision. To them, starting a doctoral program with a husband deployed and three kids three and under was all BUT a rationally sound decision. (What is rational to some may not be to others.) But alas, I plugged away.

I'd like to report that this period in my life was devoid of challenges, but we all know that it is nearly impossible within military life. But I tackled challenges differently. I breast-pumped in the car while driving home from Friday night classes and even laughed when a semitruck passed by and gave a "toot toot" after sneaking a peek at what I kindly refer to as a modern-day torture device. I began to remind myself daily of all the "could(s)" I was capable of while my husband was deployed instead of the "could not(s)."

Deployments

We all know that stress is a constant part of military life, and deployments and TDYs are part of that stress. Deployments can affect all family members differently. However, most military spouses would agree that deployments bring a high level of stress and require a great deal of perseverance.

Predeployment

In addition to the stress brought on by deployments, the predeployment process often creates unique stress. In preparation for deployment, active-duty members are required to conduct routine predeployment operations that may trigger anticipatory anxiety.[1] Consequently, the fact that today's active-duty member is expected to deploy multiple times serves as a recurrent source of stress for military families, not to mention the various emotions commonly associated with the predeployment phase.[2]

More Than a Pity Party
Kate's Story

In 2007, my husband was scheduled to deploy to Djibouti,
Africa, on an early Monday morning. We had just spent a long
weekend together preparing for an emotional goodbye, and we
were both eager to "get it over with" so we could move on to the
next challenge of the actual deployment. My husband always
preferred private goodbyes at home, so I would hold it together
until I saw his truck drive away. And then I would let myself
feel EVERYTHING for a week with a direct request of family
and friends NOT to contact me.

Why, you may ask? Well, in the past, I would often be
inundated with phone calls and emails. (Thankfully, there were
no text messages at that time.) First my mom's: "Are you OK?"
quickly followed by his mom, my dad, his brother, my sister, my
best friend, his sister—you get the point. I grew tired of saying,
"I'm OK," when it was a blatant lie but, nonetheless, my response.
I knew if I verbalized I was NOT OK that my front doorstep
would soon be crowded with family members banging down the
door. That I knew I could not handle. So they received the
programmed, automatic response because it made THEM feel
better, not me. I soon realized this was not working and asked
myself what I could possibly do to alleviate my own stress during
the predeployment phase.

What I came up with was something that worked for me. I
told all family members and friends to not contact me for one
week after he deployed. For one week, they were not allowed to
reach out, to call, to check-in. I asked them to respect my wishes.

This, I asserted, was what I needed to get through the transition. Essentially, I threw myself a solo, weeklong pity party, but it worked. I was able to work through my feelings and begin the road to accepting my new normal. Make no mistake, it wasn't easy, as there were times during that week that I craved attention from family and friends, but overall, I knew it was what I needed. And, for the record, if my husband left on a Sunday at eight a.m., then be assured all family members called, emailed, and checked in seven days later at eight a.m., but by that point, I was ready. I was comfortable and prepared for my response whether it was "I'm OK," "I'm sad," or "I'm struggling."

On this particular day, day number one of my self-thrown pity party, my husband called. That was highly unusual. I picked up the phone, "Kate, the plane is broken, and our deployment is delayed two days."

"Great!" I replied.

But what I really thought was, "Damn it!" and almost told him to go find a hotel for two days. That sounds callous, but the thought of going through it all again became one more "thing" I had to overcome.

—Kate, Air Force Spouse

Deployment

To the military spouse, the time during deployment can seem like an eternity. By necessity, the military spouse becomes the family decision-maker responsible for significant issues, as well as more inconsequential family concerns. With greater responsibility, military spouses have less time to spend with other family members, namely children. In some of my recent research, I found that during deployments military spouses experience concern associated with detachment in the parent-child relationship. Utilizing a parenting relationship questionnaire (PRQ), we found that during the active-duty member's time away from home (i.e., deployments, temporary duty assignments, and training), attachment problems commonly arose between the military spouse and child(ren).[3] Such findings suggest that during deployments, military spouses not only have an increase in daily responsibilities but that such duties invariably compete with the child(ren) for the military spouse's attention. Such is the case described by Megan below.

Each time he goes, I feel like I have less time for everything—less time for my children, less time for my other family members, less time for friends, and less time for myself. But I feel like my children take the brunt of it. Yes, I make sure all four children attend their activities. I make dinner and ask them about their day, but I don't do the little things. I forget to sit down with them and really LISTEN to their responses. Because, honestly, when they answer me, I don't hear them. I am already thinking about what I need to get done before the end of the day. I'm exhausted by the end of the day and emotionally drained. Selfishly, I avoid the emotional talks with them because sometimes I am barely holding it together. I'm afraid that if I hear the kids cry, then I will break. And I know I can't break because, in that moment, I know I'm all they have.

—Megan G., Marine Spouse

Depending on the location of a given military post, family members and close friends may be unavailable to provide support during deployments. Further aggravating the issue is the lack of familiarity with available resources or access to medical assistance. Severe personal or childhood illness can be very stressful under any circumstance but especially in an unfamiliar setting. For instance, without the help of the active-duty members, it can be extremely challenging for the military spouse to provide childcare and make doctor or medical-related appointments. On the other hand, when a spouse relocates near extended family, he or she may impact the children's educational and medical needs by moving outside of the military support network.[4] Unforeseen circumstances such as these have been shown to lead to long periods of loneliness and depression within the family during deployments.[5, 6]

Reintegration

The military defines the time when the active-duty member returns home from deployment as the "three Rs"—redeployment, reunion, and reintegration.[7] Redeployment represents the end of a mission and typically begins one month prior to the end of the deployment. During this period, spouses and children have specific expectations about how the reunion will take place. For instance, many spouses busy themselves past the point of exhaustion to ensure the house, children, and themselves are impeccable for the arrival of the active-duty member. Such efforts are an attempt to make the reunion perfect, an expectation that may be impossible to attain.

The pending return of the active-duty member can result in increased demands for the children to take more responsibility while receiving less attention (again) from the military spouse. Indeed, changes that take place during deployment may result in conflicting feelings about the military member's return.[8]

The reunion is when the active-duty member physically returns. Reunion activities take no more than a few hours or days, depending on base or unit activities employed in welcoming home the deployed service member. Depending on the length of deployment, this stage of reintegration may involve observable changes. For instance, the returning spouse may become aware of physical changes in various family members. For example, he or she may see a child walk for the first time, notice a missing tooth, or realize how tall his or her child has grown. Such changes may be stressful for the military member since he or she can see the physical impact deployment has had on his or her children. Aside from the physical and developmental changes in the children, there may also be a perceivable change in the military spouse. In this regard, such matters as weight lost or gained may have a significant impact on the effort to reestablish intimacy in the relationship.[7]

As defined by the Air Force, reintegration is the process of adjusting to a new normal that can take a few days or months. Following deployment, military families face unavoidable challenges, and most military spouses are believed to go through the following phases of reintegration: (a) honeymoon phase, (b) disillusionment, (c) anger, (d) acceptance, and (e) a new normal.[9] In 2008, two researchers, Bowling and Sherman, researched these critical stages of reintegration and presented possible actions necessary to support military families during this period of time.[10] Specific tasks associated with successful reintegration include role definitions, expectations, labor division, managing emotions, recreating a new form of intimacy, and creating shared meaning. Even with these proactive actions, military families are seldom prepared for the physical or psychological impact deployment may have upon their family.

Welcome Home?
Kate's Story, Continued

My husband's deployment to Djibouti was extended by two months, so by the time he returned home, I was more than ready. The prepared sign of: "Welcome Home, Happy Birthday!" was crossed out to "Welcome home, Happy Valentine's Day!" until finally it just became "Welcome Home!" I had painted most of the walls in our home (one of my coping skills); I made curtains and rearranged almost everything, which he later told me drove him crazy. I remember thinking I wanted to make his homecoming perfect but was struggling to know what "perfect" was. Had I changed too much? Did I change enough? Would the changes affect us?

I drove up north with our two dogs, dropped them off at my in-laws' house, and went to pick him up from the airport. I had carefully picked out my outfit, a new pencil skirt and a white blouse. When we returned to his parent's house to get the dogs, our golden retriever lost it when he saw my husband. If I ever doubted the bond of man and dog, it was completely refuted that day, as I had never heard such visceral sounds from an animal. We had dinner at his parents' house before we headed back home. As we entered our home, I was hit by an intense wave of nausea. Resolute that it must have been food poisoning from the takeout, my husband called his parents and discovered no one else was sick, just me. I was sick the entire night and then riddled with guilt. What a shitty welcome home. I recovered quickly the next day and soon realized the stress, anxiety, and anticipation of his return had taken a physical and emotional toll on my body. I was completely unaware that my irrational thoughts could cause such an intense, cathartic release upon his return.

As depicted in this story, even when reintegration is carefully monitored, some problems are harder to foresee than others. If left unrecognized and untreated, such issues may have a long-term impact on the family. Among the more leading areas of concern are communication, intimacy, and parenting. Communication can often be difficult to establish after a deployment. As such, a military spouse may conceal how he or she feels about deployments, drawing unspoken comparisons as to who had it harder during the deployment, puzzled as to why the active-duty member may or may not want to talk about the deployment, and questioning as to how individuals may miss being deployed or independent, respectively. Even pets may act out in response to human emotions that surface during family reunification.[11] Following deployment intimacy between partners, especially emotional intimacy, may be difficult to recapture. In 2001, military wives reported an awkwardness during reintegration, as the couple has learned to be emotionally independent during the deployment.[12] Since both spouses have had differing experiences, the couple must acknowledge that reconnecting emotionally will be difficult to reestablish after deployment. The deployment cycles entail distinct challenges, and military spouses are required to persevere. The very nature of deployments strips away your power and control. However, as in any situation, there is always a choice as to how you react and respond to stress associated with military life. While the reality of military life may remain the same, how you respond to such conditions is a matter of choice. That is, you are capable of assessing the impact, making it more bearable, and allowing yourself to be more in control of your thoughts and behaviors.

Rational Behavioral Technique 3
Thinking About Thinking

People are not upset by things but by their idea of things.
—Epictetus

It is important to have systematic, tangible tools readily available because the truth is it is extremely hard to locate these tools when you are already worn down or broken. These tools will help you learn how to work through your emotional responses systematically, to persevere, and to protect yourself and prepare for when you **DO** wear down again. Let's review the steps in Emotional Reeducation again from Chapter 2.

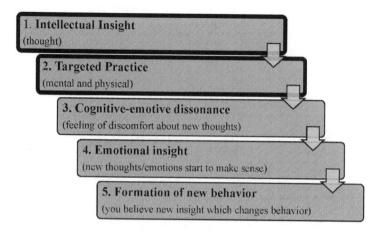

If we want to learn how to work through our emotional responses, we have to have a good understanding of our emotions. Taking a second look at the ABCs of Emotions from the last chapter, you may recall the ABCs are as follows:

ABCs of Emotions

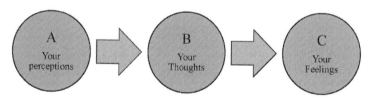

To review, according to Rational Emotive Theory, all emotions are the result of what you tell yourself about any event.[13] What this means is when you have an emotional feeling, you first perceive something (A) and then you think and believe something (B) about your perceptions.[14] Based on this belief, you have an emotion or feeling (C).

Building on the ABC theory, your emotions and feelings ultimately lead to your actions (C2). Most actions then have natural consequences or results (C3).

Thoughts + Feelings + Actions = Consequences

Figure 8. Adapted from Maultsby, M.C. (1990). *You and Your Emotions.* Self-Help Books Division: Kentucky.

Let's see how the ABC Theory of Emotions might apply to the example of military deployments.

Positive Thoughts

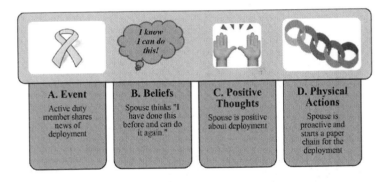

A. Event	B. Beliefs	C. Positive Thoughts	D. Physical Actions
Active duty member shares news of deployment	Spouse thinks "I have done this before and can do it again."	Spouse is positive about deployment	Spouse is proactive and starts a paper chain for the deployment

Figure 9. Lowe, K. 2019. "The ABCs of **Positive** Emotional Feelings." Thrive On, LLC.

Negative Thoughts

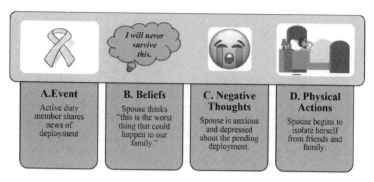

Figure 10. Lowe, K. 2019. "The ABCs of **Negative** Emotional Feelings." Thrive On, LLC.

Neutral Thoughts

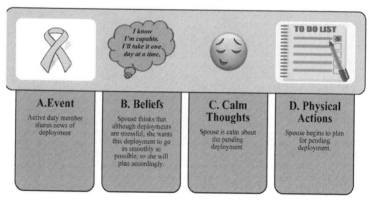

Figure 11. Lowe, K. 2019. "The ABCs of **Neutral** Emotional Feelings." Thrive On, LLC.

According to the ABC Theory of Emotions, all emotions are learned and consist of thoughts, feelings, and actions. What the ABC Theory of Emotions shows us is that we have a choice about how we perceive, feel, and act when faced with everyday events.

Three Paths of Emotions: Positive, Negative, and Neutral

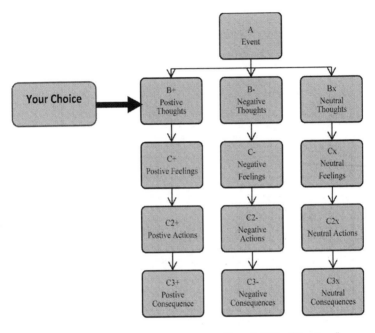

Figure 12. Lowe, K. 2019. "Positive, Negative, Neutral ABCs of Emotions."
Thrive On, LLC.

Looking at the example above, it is clear that, as military spouses, we have very little control over the events that affect our lives. But we certainly can have control over how we feel and, in turn, react to these events. Below, we'll see that it's not the events themselves that cause our feelings. Instead, it's our thoughts (positive, negative, or neutral) about the events that influence how we feel and act.

(1) **Positive** thoughts about a pending deployment create positive feelings and let you take charge of actions. "I have done this before, and **I CAN** do this

again!" Positive thoughts can lead to proactive actions, such as making lists of fun things you can do, projects you can accomplish, setting up a countdown calendar until your spouse returns, and planning monthly adventures to keep you busy.

(2) **Negative** thoughts about a pending deployment lead to angry or depressed feelings and often irrational and/or isolating actions. "This is the **worst thing** that has happened to our family, and I will never be able to do this six-month deployment." "Awfulizing" the situation often leads to resentment toward your active duty spouse, pulling away from family and friends, and/or self-medicating with alcohol, shopping, or eating.

(3) **Neutral** thoughts about a pending deployment lead to calmer feelings and planned-out actions. "I know this is going to be hard, but **I will** find a way through this deployment." These balanced thoughts can lead to healthy habits, such as a new exercise routine, counseling support, reaching out to friends, journaling, and maybe this book study!

If you are continually evaluating your thoughts and behaviors, you can begin to naturally notice when they are positive, negative, or neutral. This is not easy and will take some time and practice. The following exercises will help you develop concrete tools. Utilizing such tools, military spouses are more than capable of persevering. While deployments are used here as an example, they are not the only stressful experiences military spouses encounter.

Kate's physical response to her husband's return in 2009, throwing up all night, was probably due to the persistent negative thoughts she had prior to his arrival (i.e., "He probably won't like the house," "I should have done more to prepare for his return," "He won't like how I have changed," "We'll never be able to make up for our lost time together," and "The military doesn't care about how the deployment extension has affected us."). If Kate had the ability to look at her thoughts and how they were affecting her behaviors, it may have greatly reduced her overall anxiety.

Reflection Questions

(1) Do you believe you are currently persevering? Why or why not?

_____

_____

_____

_____

_____

(2) What does persevering look like, feel like, and act like to you as a military spouse?

_____

_____

_____

_____

_____

(3) Describe the most recent time you made a choice to persevere.

_____

_____

_____

_____

_____

(4) Recall a recent stressful event. Write down your thoughts and behaviors during this time.

Thoughts	Behaviors

(5) Look at the thoughts and behaviors you wrote above. Circle the thoughts and behaviors that are positive. Draw a line through the ones that are negative. Leave the ones that are neutral. Did you have more positive, negative, or neutral thoughts and behaviors? Describe why below. Share with your group.

_____

_____

_____

_____

_____

_____

_____

Exercise

(1) Start to practice the ABCs of Emotions. Write/draw your own comic strip below based on YOUR CURRENT stress in the military. If you can't think of one, then pick a scenario listed below.

- Your closest friend just told you he/she is PCSing next month.

- Your spouse (active duty member) misses your child's birthday or your anniversary.

- Your landlord just informed you they won't renew your lease, and you will have to move to a new home in the same area.

- Your mother is ill, and you can't go home to be with her because your spouse is TDY. You have no one to watch your children or your pets.

The ABCs of Positive Emotional Feelings

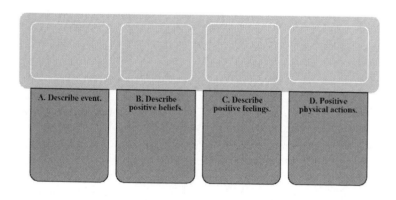

A. Describe event.	B. Describe positive beliefs.	C. Describe positive feelings.	D. Positive physical actions.

The ABCs of Negative Emotional Feelings

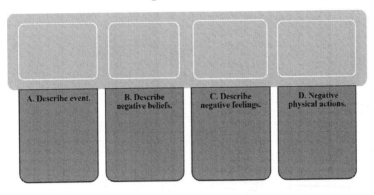

A. Describe event.	B. Describe negative beliefs.	C. Describe negative feelings.	D. Negative physical actions.

The ABCs of Neutral Emotional Feelings

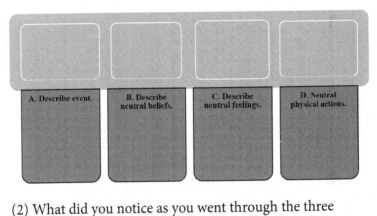

A. Describe event.	B. Describe neutral beliefs.	C. Describe neutral feelings.	D. Neutral physical actions.

(2) What did you notice as you went through the three different types of emotions? Was one comic harder than another? Why or why not?

_____

_____

_____

_____

_____

Sources

1. McAndrew, L., D'Andrea, E., Lu, S., Abbi, B., Ya, G., Engel, C. and Quigley, K. 2013. "What Predeployment and Early Postdeployment Factors Predict Health Function After Combat Deployment: A Prospective Longitudinal Study of Operation Enduring Freedom (OEF)/Operation Iraqi Freedom (OIF) Soldiers." *Health and Quality of Life Outcome*, 11, 73–82.

2. Solomon, Z. 1993. *Combat Stress Reaction: The Enduring Toll of War*. Plenum Publishing Corporation: New York.

3. Lowe, K., Adams, K., Browne, B. and Hinkle, K. 2012. "The Impact of Military Deployments on Family Relationships." *Journal of Family Studies*, 18, 17–27.

4. Park, N. 2011. "Military Children and Families: Strengths and Weaknesses During Peace and War." *American Psychologist*, 66, 65–72.

5. Mansfield, A. J., Kaufman, J. F., Marshall, S.W., Gaynes, B. N., Morrissey, J. P. and Engel, C.C. 2010. "Deployment and the Use of Mental Health Services Among US Army Wives." *New England Journal of Medicine*, 362, 101–9.

6. United States Medicine. 2009. "Department of Defense Reaches Out to Children of Soldiers." Retrieved from www.us-medicine.com/Department-of-Defense-Reaches-Out-to-Children-of-Soldiers

7. Military One Source. 2014. "Military Deployment Guide: Preparing You and Your Family for the Road Ahead." Retrieved from www.militaryonesource.mil/1238/project percent20documents/

8. Ross, A., and DeVoe, E. 2014. "Engaging Military Parents in Home-Based Reintegration Program: A Consideration of Strategies." *Health and Social Work*, 39, 47–54.

9. Veterans Benefits Administration. 2006. "Compensation and Pension Benefits Among Veterans Deployed to the Global War on

Perseverance: Make Your Setback a Comeback | 81

Terror." Retrieved from www.gwu.edu/nsarchiv/news/20061010/document02.pdf.

10. Bowling, U. and Sherman, M. 2008. "Welcoming Them Home: Supporting Service Members and Their Families in Navigating the Tasks of Reintegration." *Professional Psychology: Research and Practice*, 39, 451–458.

11. Military 2014. "Deployment: An Overview." Retrieved from www.military.com/deployment/deploymentoverview.html?comp=7000023443512andrank=1

12. Pincus, S., House, H., Christenson, J. and Adler, L. 2001. "The Emotional Cycles of Deployment: A Military Family Perspective." *US Army Medical Department Journal*, 4, 15–23.

13. Maultsby, M.C. 1990. *Rational Behavioral Therapy*. Rational Self-Help Aids: Wisconsin.

14. Maultsby, Maxie C. Jr., and Allie Hendricks. 1974. *You and Your Emotions*. Lexington, KY: Psychiatry Outpatient Clinic, University of Kentucky Medical Center.

4

The Military Spouse
How the Hell Did I End Up Here?

*If you do not know where you came from, then you don't
know where you are, and if you don't know where you are,
then you don't know where you are going. And if you don't
know where you are going, you're probably going wrong.*
—Terry Pratchett

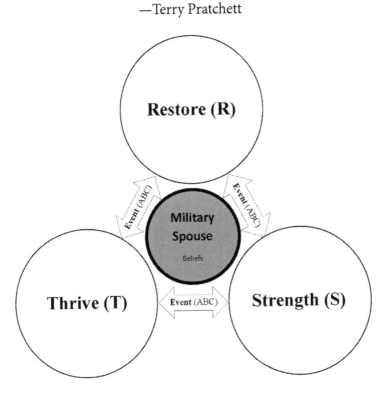

The Military Spouse

In the book *Grit: The Power of Passion and Perseverance*, Dr. Angela Duckworth explains her theory that "grit," also known as passion and perseverance, trumps talent when it comes to reaching personal goals.[1] In other words, talent matters as a baseline, but it is only a small portion of the ingredients necessary to achieve success. Our experiences as military spouses can be compared to raw talent; it is the core of who we are. As we have already discussed, we have all experienced varying degrees of stress, challenges, setbacks, successes, and failures that all shaped us into the individuals we are today. Additionally, as military spouses, we share a collective experience that is unique only to us. To break this down a little bit more, military spouses not only experience personal stress but additional stress that comes from living as a military spouse.

Individual Experiences

My Experience

As a veteran and now military spouse, I understand my views may be different than others based upon my unique past experiences. I have been profoundly shaped by the four years spent at the United States Air Force Academy (USAFA) and five and a half years of active duty prior to transitioning solely to the role of a military spouse. These years were formative, as I struggled through and overcame significant traumas that ultimately made me who I am today. Stressful events do just that; they change you and shape you (sometimes for the better and sometimes for the worse). There were crucial moments that I consciously remember choosing to focus on the pluses of my experience rather than the losses.

As such, the way I viewed the world, interpreted relationships, and defined the life I wanted to live was established during these years. I clung to the USAFA Core Values (integrity first, service before self, and excellence in all we do), for they provided motivation to persevere and overcome my past experiences, and USAFA introduced me to my soulmate, who shared these values and willingly picked up my broken pieces.

I can attest to the struggle transitioning to the role of a military spouse. While I hung up my own uniform to support my husband as he continued to wear his, I found the transition from military to civilian life to be markedly different. I recall one of my first socials after I separated from active duty in October 2006. I had recently joined my husband at Kirtland AFB in Albuquerque, NM. We had spent the last year stationed at two different bases. (I remained at Malmstrom AFB in Montana to finish my masters' degree in counseling while my husband moved to Kirtland to begin his training as a combat rescue officer.) At the time, we were going through our second year of fertility treatment, which certainly added to my unsettled emotions. My husband enjoys telling how he would quietly peer into the house after work, unsure of what he would find. He describes it as a daily "surprise!" Some days, he came home to a four-course meal, an immaculate home, and a highly functioning spouse, while other days were marked by tears and social isolation. I guess all those extra hormones made me a little unpredictable—OK, maybe even a little crazy.

Adding to our marital stress was the fact that my husband was going through "the Pipeline" in order to graduate successfully as a combat rescue officer. The Pipeline is one of the longest US Special Operations training courses, lasting almost two years, and has an attrition rate of approximately 80 percent. As such, it was exceptionally demanding of his time, as well as being physically, mentally, emotionally, and spiritually challenging. The truth be known, I found myself more alone than when we were geographically separated.

I was invited to a spouse's social event shortly after I arrived and decided to help fill this emotional and social void. I sat down on a plush sofa next to a new military spouse, and I vividly recall the first question asked.

"What do you do?"

I can remember I experienced an uncomfortable pause while I searched for the "right" answer. I was no longer wearing a uniform, and for some reason, it seemed inappropriate to start the conversation by stating I was a veteran. For some unknown reason, I was unsure if I wanted to share this part of myself with this newly defined group. At the time, I didn't have a job, although I had interviewed with several organizations and was awaiting my provisional license as a mental health professional. I wanted to be a mom in the worst way; it was one of the reasons I had decided to separate from the military, but without being pregnant, or even close, it seemed ridiculous to say I was "hoping to be a stay-at-home mom." Being pumped full of hormones, I was afraid that the mere mention of trying to get pregnant would elicit an emotional meltdown.

I silently mumbled with an uncomfortable chuckle, "Oh, you know, just a stay-at-home wife," and instantly hated myself for saying it. Surprisingly, given so many personal and professional attributes, I chose not to divulge my accomplishments. Rather the question of "Who are you?" made me think instead about who I was not! Clearly, I had not worked through my thoughts and emotions concerning my current place in life. The emotions associated with my past experiences were affecting my current happiness and my ability to transition into the role of a military spouse.

Unique Baseline of Emotions

I share this personal story because I know many people will ask, "Why is it so important to spend time discussing the past when I am struggling here in the present?" The answer is this: past experiences are a vital part of our current emotional state today—in other words, how happy we are. Dr. Martin Seligman, the author of *Learned Optimism and Authentic Happiness*, denotes that our happiness can be tied to positive emotions about the past.[2] More specifically, positive emotions about our past lead to satisfaction, contentment, fulfillment, and serenity. Negative emotions about the past can include unrelieved bitterness and vengeful anger. Bitterness as a military spouse can spread like cancer. A spouse who is bitter about missed accomplishments, incomplete career goals, and disconnection from past relationships is more likely to also be experiencing social and emotional distress.

Looking back at our ABCs of Emotions, we see that being stuck in a cycle of past negative emotions can lead to negative behaviors. Gerald Corey, in his book *The Art of Integrative Counseling*, contends that "insight can be a vehicle that enables clients to relinquish old behaviors from the past that intrude into the present."[3] Past behavior patterns, both good and bad, are repeated in the present. However, if you better understand the root of such behavior, then you can make a conscious choice as to whether or not you want to continue those behaviors. That being said, reflecting on your past does not mean you are free of the behaviors it brought with it, but it gives you the freedom to change the future.

Seligman cautions that "insufficient appreciation and savoring of the good events in your past along with an overemphasis of the bad ones are the two culprits that undermine serenity, contentment, and satisfaction."[2] Take and reflect on the following question: how satisfied do you believe you are right now with your life? To help you assess your current satisfaction with life, I encourage you to complete the scale below.

The Life Satisfaction Scale

Using the 1–7 scale below, mark how much you agree with each statement below.[2]

7 = Strongly agree
6 = Agree
5 = Slightly agree
4 = Neither agree nor disagree
3 = Slightly disagree
2 = Disagree
1 = Strongly disagree

___ In most ways, my life is close to ideal.
___ The conditions of my life are excellent.
___ I am completely satisfied with my life.
___ So far, I have gotten the important things I want in my life.
___ If I could live my life over, I would change nothing.

___ Total

30–35 Extremely satisfied, much above average
25–29 Very satisfied, above average
20–24 Somewhat satisfied, average for American adults

15–19 Slightly dissatisfied, a bit below average

10–14 Dissatisfied, clearly below average

5–9 Very dissatisfied, much below average

Figure 13. The Life Satisfaction Scale. Seligman, M. E. (2002). *Authentic Happiness: Using the New Positive Psychology to Realize Your Potential for Lasting Fulfillment.* New York: The Free Press.

Your score on the life satisfaction survey isn't the point but, rather, a marker to provide you with a baseline. RBT holds that emotional feelings are a direct result of what people think about events in their lives. In other words, *emotional responses are NOT caused by external events but rather result from our beliefs about those events.* If these past experiences cause us to continue to experience negative emotions and behavior, it can be detrimental to our emotional and mental well-being.

The late Steven Covey, the author of the *7 Habits of Highly Effective People,* illustrated these concepts quite eloquently.[4] He recalled a man who sat down on the subway one Sunday morning and allowed his children to roam wildly about the car, screaming and jumping on seats. Covey was annoyed by the man's lack of interaction with, and discipline of, his children.

Perplexed, he finally asked, "Sir, your children are really disturbing a lot of people; I wonder if you could try to control them just a little more."

The man replied, "You're right. I should do something, but we just came from the hospital where their mother died about an hour ago, and I guess they don't know how to handle it. I guess I don't know how to handle it either." Covey recounted how in a manner of seconds, his mental concept of the children and father's behavior shifted. He saw things completely differently. In that moment, he began to think and feel differently, which lead him to act differently. His irritation vanished and was replaced with compassion. Acting on more positive thoughts and emotions, he offered to help the man instead of turning away.[4]

Military Spouse Experiences

The basic premise of RBT is that past experiences and beliefs create our current emotions and behaviors. An important extension of this principle is that "today will be your past tomorrow." In short, in order to deal with your emotions, you must NEXT think about current events.

Finding My New Identity
Lucy's Story

After my (now) husband proposed, I was ecstatic to get back to work the following Monday to show off my new ring and tell my coworkers about the romantic proposal. I told them all about how my fiancé proposed a few days before he moved to Japan and how sweet it would be when he came back for his bride a few months later so that we could get married and start our lives together overseas. That's when one of my closest friends asked the daunting question, "What about your career?"

I spent six years in college, obtaining undergraduate and graduate degrees in speech pathology. Since that time, I had worked my way into a lead therapist position at a hospital specializing in neurological injuries—also known as my dream job.

I responded with a complete lie, "Oh, I'll find something I'm just as passionate about!" Wrong.

A few months later, I said "I do" at the altar in Fairhope, Alabama, and in less than thirty-six hours, I was on a plane heading overseas to begin my journey as a military spouse. I left my cherished family and friends and put a hold on my beloved career in Florida. I was excited about new challenges and experiences. I was excited about the unknown of living in a foreign country (I had never even flown outside of the US before I got married) and excited to see what job opportunities I could find in Japan. How different could it be?

I didn't come from a military family, so when I attended my first newcomers' briefing in Okinawa and someone yelled "a-ten-HUT!" when a man with a shiny rank entered the room, I seemed to be the only person in the full auditorium who didn't know what was going on. Of course, I was the last person to stand up, while my heart sank with the realization that I was now in a foreign culture in more ways than one. That's when it hit me just how much I did not know about being a military spouse. I felt very alone. I spent the first few months looking for jobs, trying to make new friends, and desperately trying to figure out how to be a military spouse. I cried, prayed, journaled, and called my family frequently. I didn't know how to interact with a culture full of acronyms and military customs. I didn't know the "rules" of being a military spouse. My husband tried to calm my fears and quiet my insecurities, but it wasn't until I immersed myself in the military spouse culture that things really changed for me.

I spent most of my time overseas establishing my new identity as a military spouse and figuring out the advantages and disadvantages that come with the title. I quickly learned the acronyms TDY and PCS and figured out the differences between the various branches of the military. I learned that no matter how resilient military spouses appear to be, it's still OK for us to feel discouraged when the mission takes priority over family time or when last-minute TDYs disrupt anniversary plans. I discovered the beauty of homecomings after months apart. I learned how to build strong friendships with spouses quickly. I learned to stand at attention when the colonel walks into the room at the promotion ceremony. Most importantly, I learned that I am not alone and many military spouses feel exactly like I do.

—Lucy Witzig, Air Force Spouse

Cultural Impact

Lucy's experience illustrates the social-emotional difficulty of adjusting to a new culture. Indeed, the military has a distinct culture of its own. Lucy's experiences illustrate the difficulties, both socially and emotionally, of adjusting to this culture— that is, the military has its own unique social, demographic, and personal constructs.[5]

These unique military social constructs consist of elements shared by individuals who speak a particular dialect, live in the same geographical location at the same time, and share norms, roles, values, associations, and ways of categorizing experience described as "subjective culture."[6] A concrete visual representation of culture was developed by the Dutch researcher Geert Hofstede. He developed his well-known "Cultural Onion," defined as "the collective programming of the mind that distinguishes the members of one group or category from another."[7]

The Cultural Onion

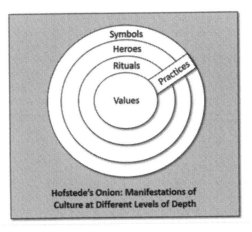

Figure 14. The Cultural Onion. Hofstede, G. (1991). *Cultures and Organizations: Software of the Mind*. London: McGraw-Hill.

The US Military clearly displays cultural paradigms, such as a unique dialect, social ranking, norms, roles, symbols, values, rituals, practices, and associations. As military spouses, we become part of this unique culture the minute we pledged to stand beside, for better or worse, our military spouse. Unfortunately, most of us are not prepared for the drastic impact of this new culture we've entered.

The most obvious example of this "new culture" is seen in the unique language that eventually becomes second nature to military families. In recent studies, mental health trainees struggled to provide clinical care to military veterans because they didn't understand the distinct language common to the military.[8] For example, the mental health trainees did not know basic military terminology, such as R & R (leave), Article 15 (disciplinary action), or the Air Force Specialty Code (AFSC for your job description). The authors reported that this lack of understanding military terminology could lead to an inaccurate diagnosis for some military veterans.[8] In this regard, military terminology not only provides communication between military members but also enhances the mental health professional's ability to understand the unique, dynamic, common language it brings to the relationship.

Acronym Hell
Rebecca's Story

I remember driving through the base in San Antonio for the first time to visit my husband at work. After I weaved through the concrete blockades, I was stopped at the gate and was told to present my ID. I frantically searched my wallet ("Damn, how I wished I were more organized,"), found it, and showed him my California driver's license. I was quickly corrected, "Ma'am, not your driver's license, your military ID."

I went back into my wallet to search and found the newly laminated ID and proudly presented it to the gate guard. First hesitating, then deciding the guard seemed kind and helpful, I asked him for directions to my husband's squadron. I was so wrong; the wicked gate guard inundated me with completely foreign acronyms: "Ma'am ("Why did he have to say it again?"), Unit AFSC, BX, Annex, ma'am (yes, again), PCS, VOQ, TLF, commissary, and ma'am (for a fourth time)." I shook my head up and down appropriately as if I understood and then asked for a base map to save what little dignity I had left. It took me forty-five minutes to find my husband's squadron that day, well past our planned lunch, and I remember feeling I had entered into some strange, warped reality.

—Rebecca, Air Force Spouse

The influence of the cultural constructs on active duty members, as well as their families, have significant implications. Recent research suggests that members perceive the need for psychological services to be a negative stigma on the service record of an airman or soldier. In a study of 731 service members diagnosed with a mental health disorder, 65 percent indicated that they believed treatment would be viewed as a weakness. Additionally, 59 percent expressed concern that their special units would have less confidence in them as a result of being informed of their mental illness. Finally, 63 percent feared that their chain of command would treat them differently, knowing they suffered from a mental disorder.

Such findings are not surprising since military veterans have long harbored negative feelings toward mental health treatment. These attitudes have been ingrained through years of active-duty service. In one case study involving a male military veteran, researchers reported that the veteran's unwillingness to seek mental health help not only led to altered symptom presentation but erroneously shaped his course of treatment.[9] The United Services Organization (USO), following up on mental health concerns, reported in 2018 that military spouses continue to be hesitant to seek mental health support because of the potential negative impact on their spouse's career or military clearances.[10] Such negative beliefs, associated with the need for clinical care, undoubtedly influence how military members and their families respond to a range of educational and mental health professionals. Yet, current research depicts a critical need for mental health services.

The Fear is Alive and Well
Nicole's Story

I had wanted and planned for a fourth child and, therefore, was taken completely by surprise when I suffered from severe post-partum after she was born. With no familial support around me, having a baby at thirty-seven turned out to be far more than I imagined. I began to fear everything: she wasn't gaining enough weight, she wasn't sleeping enough, and I didn't know when I would ever feel like myself again.

There were days, maybe even an entire week, that I didn't want to leave my home. I forgot to shower on some days and wasn't sleeping. All I did was worry, and yet, I remained unaware of how much I was struggling—that is, until one very memorable Thursday night. A close friend, who was also a military spouse, had heard that I was struggling, so she stopped by with another spouse unexpectedly to see me. I admitted to them both all the fears I was consumed with on a daily basis. The look on their faces told me what I had said was shocking, and yet, it sounded "normal" to me. My friend gently took my hand and said we were all going to the Mental Health Flight right then. They had prearranged care for my two-month-old daughter and would go with me as a walk-in to the appointment. I fought for a good hour, saying I didn't need to go, that it would hurt my husband's career, that I would be labeled as "crazy," and that it could hurt our next assignment if I was "Q coded" with mental health concerns. I pretty much tried any valid reason I could come up with to get out of going to Mental Health. But they both knew I was severely suffering, and although the reasons not to go could certainly still come true, my mental well-being was more important than the future military repercussions.

They sat with me for four hours that night. We waited to get a walk-in evening appointment, and they never left my side until I was seen by a professional psychologist. The fear of going to mental health was eased somewhat when I finally met the psychologist, who led me out of my crisis that evening. It has been a long road with many professionals involved to get me to where I am today.

Anxiety can be debilitating, as I was consumed by thoughts my anxiety controlled. It is different from depression, a difference that not many understand. So I started a support group for new moms at our next duty assignment, hoping my experience could help them. Looking back, I wish I had not feared seeking out help, but the reality is that this fear is still alive and well in our military community. We need resources that can reach our spouses when they are unable to reach out themselves.

—Nicole Fike, Air Force Spouse

As noted by both Nicole and Lucy's stories above, military spouses are undoubtedly part of a specific subculture and, as such, can suffer from unique stressors. Consequently, military spouses need better ways to cope with our stress levels and subsequent emotional distress. By reading and reflecting on the habitual emotions and irrational attitudes of RBT, the journey to defining new rational emotions and behaviors can begin.

Rational Behavioral Technique 4
Identifying Habitual Emotions and Irrational Attitudes and Beliefs

The mind is its own place, and in itself, can make Heaven of Hell, or Hell of Heaven.
—Milton

Habitual Emotions
ABCs of Emotions

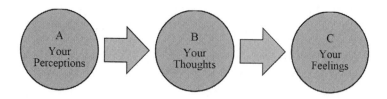

It is not uncommon for a military spouse to reach these levels of social-emotional stress in the same way time after time. I've often heard military spouses say, "I feel like I am stuck in this cycle, and I don't know how to change it." There is a scientific reason why this happens. When we think the same thought (B) about the same event (A), we get the same emotional and behavioral result (C). As normal human beings, we learn to train our brains to automatically respond. Specifically, the left brain takes the repeatedly combined thoughts and events and converts them to semipermanent beliefs. These beliefs are then taken from the left brain and formed into permanent attitudes by the right brain.[11]

Attitude and Belief Controlled Emotions
Basic ABCs of Emotions

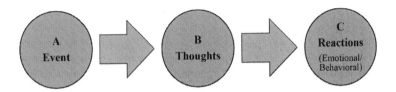

Belief Controlled Emotions

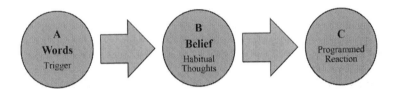

Attitude Controlled Emotions

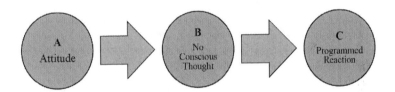

Figure 15. Adapted from Maultsby, M.C. (1990). *You and Your Emotions.*
Self-Help Books Division: Kentucky.

After the pairings of ABC (events, thoughts, and feelings) are repeated several times, beliefs and attitudes will form. Once a belief is formed (and stored in the brain), then there is no need for the actual event to take place. At this point, the words alone (not necessarily the event) can trigger the beliefs, which will then trigger specific emotional and behavioral reactions. Beliefs are then the spoken, or conscious, form of attitudes.

Deployment Fear Analogy
Programmed Response (Repeated)

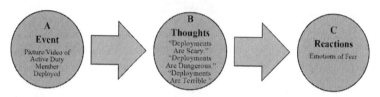

Belief Controlled Emotions

Attitude Controlled Emotions

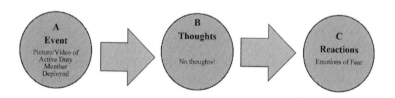

Figure 16. Lowe, K. 2019. Deployment Fear Analogy. Thrive On, LLC.

Irrational Attitudes

Our attitudes are what we believe so strongly that we don't have to think before we react to a situation. In other words, attitudes are the result of habitually pairing the same ABC pattern. As a result, many attitudes are unknowingly automatically formed and because they are not spoken, we often forget that they have formed.[12]

Unknowingly, as military spouses, we have many habitual pairings of the ABC pattern. For example, the unique demands of military service often require military spouses to function as a solo parent. Given the obligations to the military, the active duty member's role in family affairs is often reduced, which causes the military spouse to function as a single parent. This role may result in feelings of anxiety, depression, and sometimes resentment. When military spouses perceive themselves as a single parent, they are likely to experience immediate unpleasant feelings even BEFORE the experience begins. Not surprisingly, most military spouses are unaware of the automatic attitudes triggered by such situations. Recognizing this fact, it is critical for the military community to provide education, training, supportive services, and increased resources to families.

To increase your attitude awareness, start by looking at the list on the Military Attitude Identification Chart on the next page. This will help determine which unpleasant feelings are associated with your thoughts. It can also help you start to make your thoughts, feelings, and actions more rational.

Military Attitude Identification Chart

Unpleasant Feeling	Irrational Attitude	Rational Attitude	Desirable Feeling
1. Depression	• "I can't do this anymore." • "It's hopeless; nothing will ever change." • "Military life is awful."	• You can do far more than you think. • There is always hope. • Military life has positive and negative aspects.	• Calm • Concern • Disappointment • Hope • Good
2. Anxiety	• "It WOULD be awful (if he were to deploy, we were to move, etc.)."	• It wouldn't be absolutely awful. • "I'm in no physical danger." • "Nothing bad is going to happen."	• Calm • Concern
3. Anger	• "The military shouldn't have ..." • "It's not fair." • "The military just doesn't care."	• "I will accept what has happened. I don't like it, so I will ..." • "The world is not always fair. I don't like it, so I will ..." • "People/organizations are capable of making mistakes."	• Calm • Dislike • Disappointed • Motivated to change
4. Guilt	• "I shouldn't have (yelled at him/her for volunteering for a TDY)."	• "I should have because I choose to do it, and I will continue until I change, so I will ..."	• Calm • Motivated to change • Regret
5. Resentment	• "I shouldn't have to (go to all these 'mandatory' military events)."	• "I choose to. People do not 'force' me."	• Calm • Good about what I choose • Dislike
6. Hurt	• "He/she didn't do what I expected." (Come home on time for our son's birthday party.)	• "He/she doesn't have to do what I expected in order for me to be OK."	• Calm • Disappointed

Table 4. Lowe, K. (2019). "Military Attitude Identification Chart." Thrive On, LLC.

Attitudes are driven by our self-talk, as depicted in the Attitude Identification Chart above. However, because attitudes are unspoken, most individuals do not even know their own attitudes. If you can start to become aware of what attitudes are triggering your emotions, then you can gain control over your emotional and behavioral responses.

Below are six unpleasant feelings, each of which are associated with a rational script. To identify your underlying attitude, first identify which unpleasant feeling you experience the most. Then read the script associated with each unpleasant feeling to begin to form more rational attitudes. Read this script every day for a week, and note your responses at the end of this chapter.

Unpleasant Feelings Daily Script

Unpleasant Feeling	Daily Script
1. Depression/Hurt	"What I do does not change me. Sometimes I make mistakes, and sometimes I do things very well, but I'm the same person no matter what I do. Other people have a right to do what they do and to think about what they think. Other people's thoughts do not control or define my feelings. I control my thoughts, feelings, and behavior. I feel good about the things I do well and regret some things I do not do well. I accept these behaviors because I accept myself. I feel calm about myself. I feel acceptable to myself. I feel good about accepting myself."
2. Anxiety/Guilt	"I am in control of how I feel. I want to feel calm, and I feel calm now. I remember that I am a person of human dignity no matter what other people think of me or how many mistakes I make. I do not need the approval or caring of others to feel calm. Even if people do not think of me the way I would like, I can stand it. Whenever someone else (or I) does something I do not like, I remind myself that I am like everyone else; I make mistakes. I am the most important person in my life because I control my life."
3. Anger/Resentment	"The world is always as it should be at any given moment. That doesn't mean I like what is happening or what has happened or that I think it is the best. It means that everything necessary to make it happen has happened. If I do not like it, then I can do my best to change it if I choose to and prevent it from happening in the future. I will decide if I am willing to do what's necessary to get what I want. I realize that I am responsible for taking action to influence change if I want something to be different. I am calmly reminding myself of my choices as I accept the world as it is now."

Table 5. Adapted from Maultsby, M.C. (1990). *You and Your Emotions.*
Self-Help Books Division: Kentucky.

In military life, it often seems we have little control over what happens. However, we CAN take control of our attitudes. You have the choice to systematically change your irrational attitude because you now know these DRIVE our emotions.

Reflection Questions

(1) What are a few of your past experiences, prior to becoming a military spouse, that you believe continue to influence you today?

_____

_____

_____

_____

_____

_____

_____

(2) If you could rewrite one of the chapters of your life, how would you like it to go?

_____

_____

_____

_____

_____

_____

_____

(3) To what extent have your past experiences given you greater appreciation for your current challenges?

_____

_____

_____

_____

_____

_____

(4) What were your goals/dreams prior to becoming a military spouse?

_____

_____

_____

_____

_____

_____

_____

(5) What have you experienced that is unique to being a military spouse (as compared to when you were not)?

_____

_____

_____

_____

_____

_____

_____

_____

(6) What experiences have you had adjusting to the military culture? Share with your group.

_____

_____

_____

_____

_____

_____

_____

_____

Exercises

(1) What unpleasant feeling do you experience most when you have a setback? (Circle in the chart.) Why do you think you experience this feeling most often? Describe below.

Unpleasant Feeling	
1. Depression	
2. Anxiety	
3. Anger	
4. Guilt	
5. Resentment	
6. Hurt	

(2) Work through the following chart to help target underlying attitudes. Remember, they may be underlying and hard to identify. Discuss it with a friend or with your group.

Unpleasant Feeling	Irrational Attitude	Rational Attitude	Desirable Feeling

(3) Read the script in the chapter associated with your unpleasant feeling identified in the Attitude Identification Chart once per day, every day, until you meet as a group again (or for approximately a week if you are working through this book alone).

Day 1. Read through the script associated with your identified unpleasant feeling.

_____

_____

_____

_____

_____

Day 2. Read through the script associated with your identified unpleasant feeling. Write below what ideas you DISAGREE with.

_____

_____

_____

_____

_____

Day 3. Read through the script associated with your unpleasant identified feeling and write below what ideas you AGREE with.

_____

_____

_____

_____

_____

Day 4. Read through the script associated with your identified unpleasant feelings and write below events and examples of when you have experienced these feelings.

_____

_____

_____

_____

_____

Day 5. Read through the script and write below events/ examples from your daily lives in which you could have applied a rational attitude in the script.

_____

_____

_____

_____

_____

Day 6. Read through the script and write below events from YOUR daily life in which you have gained new insights from this chapter.

_____

_____

_____

_____

Day 7. Read through the script associated with your
unpleasant feeling, and review your notes.

_____

_____

_____

_____

_____

Sources

1. Duckworth, Angela. 2016. *Grit: The Power of Passion and Perseverance.* Toronto, Ontario: HarperCollins.

2. Seligman, M. E. 2002. *Authentic Happiness: Using the New Positive Psychology to Realize Your Potential for Lasting Fulfillment.* New York: The Free Press.

3. Corey, G. 2001. The Art of Integrative Counseling. Belmont: Thomson Brooks/Cole.

4. Covey, S. 2004. *7 Habits of Highly Effective People.* New York: Simon and Schuster.

5. Triandis, H. C. 1972. *The Analysis of Subjective Culture.* New York: Wiley.

6. Triandis, H. C., Bontempo, R., Leung, K., and Hui, C. H. 1990. "A Method for Determining Cultural, Demographic, and Person Constructs." *Journal of Cross-Cultural Psychology*, 21, 302–318.

7. Hofstede, G. 1991. *Cultures and Organizations: Software of the Mind.* London: McGraw-Hill.

8. Storm, T., Gavian, M., Possis, E., Loughlin, J., Bui, T., Linardatos, E., Leskela, J., and Siegel, W. 2012. "Cultural and Ethical Considerations When Working with Military Personnel and Veterans:

A Primer for VA Training Programs." *Training and Education In Professional Psychology*, 6, 67–75.

9. Hoge, C. W., Castro, C. A., Messer, S. C., McGurk, D., Cotting, D. I., and Koffman, R. L. 2004. "Combat Duty in Iraq and Afghanistan, Mental Health Problems and Barriers to Care." *New England Journal of Medicine*, 351, 13–22.

10. United Services Organization (USO) 2018. "The Backbone of Our Military: Perceptions and Experiences from Modern Military Spouses." Arlington: USO, Inc.

11. Maultsby, M.C. 1990. *Rational Behavioral Therapy*. Rational Self-Help Aids: Wisconsin.

12. Maultsby, Maxie C. Jr., and Allie Hendricks. 1974. *You and Your Emotions*. Lexington, KY: Psychiatry Outpatient Clinic, University of Kentucky Medical Center.

5

Restoration
Real People are Never Perfect, and Perfect People are Never Real

Even when we're in great distress, joy can still be found in moments we seize and moments we create. Cooking. Dancing. Hiking. Praying. Driving. Singing Billy Joel songs off-key. All of these can provide relief from pain. And when these moments add up, we find that they give us more than happiness; they also give us strength.
—Sheryl Sandberg, *Option B*

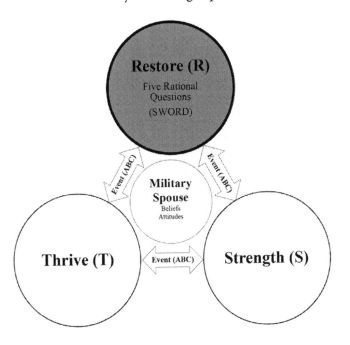

Restoration Defined

Stress remains constant, setbacks are inevitable, and perseverance is a choice, but what if you **think** you are not resilient
and cannot bounce back? What if you **believe** the weight of
your stress is crippling? What if the **thought** of trying to get
out of bed is overwhelming? Such thoughts are common
among military spouses, yet thoughts and beliefs like these go
unrecognized because of the fear of saying, "I'm not OK."
Since many military spouses often fear saying they are "not
OK," it remains extremely difficult to identify who would
benefit from social-emotional support and those who need
professional intervention. This is why the restoration stage is
so critical to the well-being of military spouses.

*Military spouses must begin to relieve their own
emotional stress with specific RBT tools if unable
or unwilling to attend targeted interventions
or receive professional help.*

The restoration stage is the process of "recovering and
rehabilitating after damage to our former condition." During
the restoration stage, a universal language is established for
spouses to use while they recover from stressful situations. It
serves to validate the stress and is an important first step
toward social-emotional well-being. This important stage
helps us to address individual stressors rather than allowing
social-emotional conditions to lead to debilitating anxiety and
depression. Specifically, the restoration phase helps military
spouses to rationally inoculate themselves against prolonged
stress or an isolated traumatic event. This critical pause allows
military spouses to consciously examine their thoughts,

emotions, and subsequent behaviors. The better these components of social-emotional well-being are understood, the greater the OVERALL social-emotional health of the military spouse.

Restoration is a critical first stage in the military spouses's social-emotional reeducation—one in which they will spend a large portion of their personal and family lives.

Unbreakable

My Experience

At my last military spouse social in Okinawa, a group of fourteen ladies gathered at a local pizza place on the Sea Wall. It is probably one of my favorite spots in Okinawa. If you are there at just the right time, you are able to witness the sky painted in luminous arrays of colors ranging from pinks, to purples, to oranges, to yellows, and sometimes to even burnt red at sunset. That night was bittersweet. We had to say goodbye to four women at this event, all of us going in different directions. This was the last night we would all be together, and as always, it elicited a vast array of emotions, which eloquently fit the sky that night.

As part of our squadron's parting gifts for spouses, they were each presented with a silver bracelet stamped with the longitude and latitude coordinates of the unit location, as well as their initials. It was a way for them to remember not only their time in Okinawa but also their time being part of a unique squadron and rescue mission. Past spouses choose to either wear it proudly on their wrists or tuck it away into personal jewelry boxes so it can be looked at periodically, hopefully eliciting joy and happiness.

After the bracelets and flowers were set aside and pizza and sushi were served (an odd combination, but we were, after all, in Japan), the spouses comfortably fell into various conversations based on their location at the long rectangular table. In my group of four spouses, they kindly asked how I was handling the stress of the move. Luckily, minus a few minor bumps with late orders setting back our pack-out dates, I reported that our move was going well. However, I shared that my six-year-old son was probably struggling the most.

I shared how my husband and I had decided I would stay back to manage the pack out of our household items while he took our three children to the Japanese Air Rescue base for their annual summer event. We thought it would be a good distraction for them from the pending move and knew they would have one last night with their belongings before they were scheduled to load the truck the next day.

The Japanese movers arrived at nine a.m. with five workers and quickly went to work, delegated in five areas of the house as my husband departed with the children. To my amazement, they packed out our house and loaded it onto the moving truck in ten hours. This is pretty extraordinary, as the team had to pack out 15,000 pounds of household items, prep the shipment for transport halfway around the world, and crate it onto two moving trucks. In fact, they were so fast that I had to check several times to see if our dog, Buddy, was still underfoot, as we had experienced in the past that movers can often pack random, odd, crazy things when you are not looking, like trash from your kitchen trashcan, parts to refrigerators that were staying with the house, plants, and dirty laundry—to name a few. So it definitely took the children by surprise when they returned at four p.m. to see that the house was empty—completely empty.

They each ran into their individual rooms to check out their new reality and saw that the only visible furniture left in the house was the tatami mats and air mattresses that I had laid out for all of us in the master bedroom. The temporary furniture would not be delivered for another two days because the movers had finished ahead of schedule. We all had a rough night's sleep, but my son, Gabriel's, was probably the worst. He woke me up about three a.m. with his face a mere inch from mine and his whisper of "MOM."

After my heart rate returned to semi-normal, he confessed, "Mom, I'm so sorry. I wet the bed," and he started to cry. Thus began a long two weeks where we had to convince our son that it wasn't his fault that he had to wear pull-ups again, that he was still a good boy, and that we all struggle in different ways when we have to move and leave our home.

After recounting my story to the four other spouses surrounding me, one spouse interjected, "But you're a psychologist, so I'm sure you handled it and got over it quickly." Wow, was she wrong. It broke my heart to hear my son cry and to watch him regress through this move when he had worked so hard the past year to "graduate" out of pull-ups. Yes, maybe being a psychologist gave me access to quick tools, but the emotional stress I felt during those two weeks was as real as any other spouse. I couldn't stop thinking about how much we were putting him through.

Although her intent was clearly not malicious, it confirmed what I continued to encounter with military spouses—a deeply rooted stigma that there were certain military spouses who "should be" better postured to handle the stress associated with military life: the military spouse who is a psychologist, the seasoned military spouse who navigated this life cycle for twenty-six years, or maybe the military spouse who spoke at resiliency weekends and initiated nonprofit organizations for spouses. Outwardly, these spouses appear to adjust and bounce back well, but let me assure you that outside appearances or demographics don't always match internal feelings and emotions.

I've always loved watching the movie *Unbreakable* by M. Night Shyamalan, where a common man (David Dunn) is capable of superhuman strength coupled with a form of extrasensory perception. Although wildly unrealistic, I enjoyed immersing myself in a fictitious world where truly in-destructible human beings exist. Why? Because I think there are times when we all wish we were unbreakable. There is a part of all of us that wishes we could survive the most intense situations and walk away unscathed. However, the reality of a military spouse is one in which life presents unique mental, emotional, and physical stress, which if left untended, can lead to significant social-emotional distress.

Distraction or Destruction?
Amy's Story

I am an expert at distracting myself. When I get stressed, I just add more to my plate so I don't have to think about it. I take on a new project at work or I volunteer for another committee or at my kids' school—the more the better. I run around so I have less time to sit because when I sit all I do is think about how much I miss him and my family. I do it out of avoidance, which creates more stress, until eventually everything comes crashing down. I get sick or pure exhaustion takes over, and I find myself hiding in the bathroom, crying on the floor. I just don't know how to stop it because it is the only way I know how.

—Amy, Marine Spouse

I want you to pause for a moment and answer a few simple questions. First, I want to envision the military spouse at the clinical levels of stress that we discussed in Chapter 2. Now, ask yourself the following questions.

- Has he/she been part of the military for a few months, or is he/she a seasoned spouse?

- Has the active duty member spent the past twenty-four months away from home or at home for twenty-four months?
- Is the family part of the Air Force, Army, Navy, Marines, or Coast Guard?
- How many children are in that family?
- Do any of the family members have special needs?

In the space below, describe the military spouse you envisioned based on the criteria above.

_____

_____

_____

_____

_____

_____

_____

_____

_____

_____

_____

_____

Stress and Military Spouse Demographics

Remember the statistics presented in Chapter 2 (27 percent of military spouses could potentially be at elevated levels of stress and 20 percent at a higher, clinically significant level of stress)? One in four of all military spouses could be suffering from clinical levels of stress like the spouse you described above. However, research suggests that military spouse stress does not discriminate. Which spouses are suffering more? This was determined by investigating six specific variables as potentially significant contributors to clinical levels of stress among military spouses.[1]

Military Spouse Demographics

Variable	Definition
1. Branch of service	Air Force, Navy, and Army
2. Gender	Male or female
3. Length of service	How long the active duty member has been part of the military
4. Time away from home	Deployments, TDYs, and training time in the past twenty-four months
5. Exceptional Family Members Program	Families with special medical or educational needs
6. Number of children family	How many children in the

Table 6. Lowe, K. 2019. "Military Spouse Demographics of Research." Thrive On, LLC.

Results

My research revealed no difference between stress levels for all but one of these variables. ALL military spouses are vulnerable to stress. For example, the male spouses who were interviewed did not exhibit significantly higher stress levels than female spouses. Is this surprising to you?

Same Stress, Different Look
Hakeem's Story

Being a male and also being a military spouse is a totally different dynamic. Personally, I feel like my stress level is different from female spouses but not higher. If you look at the majority of military spouses, they are primarily female, and the fact is, we think differently than them. Males, by nature, believe we are the ones who need to make the money and not stay at home. For me, that mindset did consume me at times because I couldn't find work and was forced into the supporting spouse role. The mental fatigue was hard, and I struggled in the military spouse community to make connections with only females present. You have to be willing to partner up with other female spouses because the fact is, you won't always get that male camaraderie you may crave. Military life is stressful, regardless of your gender; it just feels and looks different on all of us.
—Hakeem Walton, Army Spouse

As for the length of service, it has also been found the stress levels of spouses who have been part of the military for many years (twenty to twenty-six years) were not significantly different than the spouses who had been part of the military for one year. The stress levels were the SAME.

Military spouses are part of this unique culture from the moment the active duty member raises their right hand. From that moment on, stress becomes a part of their lives. Many military spouses grow accustomed to stress as part of their military experience. Literature is contradictory in this respect. Studies have indicated that as military families increase service time, they become more resilient through training and education.[2] However, research also suggests that as service length increases, the military families begin to feel the effects of operational fatigue.[3] My finding suggests that military spouses with only a few years of service experience stress levels similar to those families with numerous years of service. That is, the military spouses' overall stress levels remain constant, regardless of the length of service, as depicted by Jennifer, a seasoned spouse below.

Stress is My Constant
Jennifer's Story

It's hard to believe that I have been a military spouse for twenty-two years. I've seen lots of changes in our military world, but the one thing that has remained constant is my level of stress. If anything, my stress has gone up; it's a persistent nagging in the back of my mind. At the beginning of my marriage, the stressors were different. I would worry about my marriage being strong enough to survive the last-minute deployments, missing that weekly call, or that our kids would struggle with moving every few years. Now, the struggles are worrying if my spouse will finally reach the point of exhaustion, if my kids will find their own path to happiness, and how I will fit into this current military world.

Being a seasoned spouse makes me feel like I should have all the answers: for example, how to move through the PCS and deployment cycles seamlessly. The only answer I am assured of is to ask for help. When we recently moved back to the States after four years overseas, I still had to manage the pack out, plan pet travel, TLF living, change of command, more TLF living, in processing, buying a car, new cell phones, visiting family we haven't seen in a bit, my husband out processing for a 365-day deployment, and the kids and I finally returning to our "new" base. We settled into our TLF to wait five long months for our house on base to open while my husband worked fourteen-hour days in a place that is on the news daily. All of those stressors are still hard, even after twenty-two years of experience as a spouse.

After serving as a leadership spouse, making many baby meals and gifts, and providing support and counseling for some amazing families, it's so hard to be the one to ask for help. Being the one with the answers or serving as the go-to person, it's easy to hide behind a facade that says, "We're OK." Asking for help never gets easy. People offer to help, but it's hard to take them up on it. I often realize we find the most joy and fulfillment in helping others. Learning to accept help is more difficult for me than giving help. My circle of peers is smaller now, and I've been the helper for so long, asking for help feels odd. I feel like everyone expects me to have the answers and know-how to fix everything.

—Jennifer, Air Force Spouse

As a final example, the stress levels of military spouses with an active duty member home for twenty-four months was no different than the stress levels of spouses where the active duty member had been away for the entire twenty-four months. Time away did not significantly impact overall stress levels for military spouses, presumably because stress is a constant within military families. Time away from home did not have a significant effect on emotional stress, due to the unique nature of military service.[4] Many active-duty members identify military service as a calling, not a nine-to-five job, with many consumed by their dedication to their military service. As honorable as such service may be, active-duty members' level of commitment and dedication invariably places significant demands on the spouse that may materialize in the form of clinical levels of stress.

The Exception: Exceptional Family Member Program (EFMP)

In the early 1980s, the military established a program titled the Exceptional Family Member Program (EFMP) to help military families who have members with special educational or medical needs. This program supports children, spouses, or dependent adults of active-duty personnel. According to EFMP guidelines, there are four distinct categories by which an individual can qualify for services. These categories are: (1) require special medical services for a chronic condition, such as asthma, attention deficit disorder, diabetes, multiple sclerosis, etc., (2) receive ongoing services from a medical specialist, (3) have significant behavioral health concerns, (4) or receive early intervention or special education services through a specialized education program or a specialized family service plan. Once enrolled in the EFMP program, families can receive any or all of the following: information on community services, related education, referrals to other professional providers, local school and early intervention services, case management, and specialized plans.[5] According to the 2018 Defense Primer Report, approximately 137,000 military families receive support from EFMP. (US Army military families get 40 percent, the largest share to receive EFMP support.[6]) Unfortunately, this percentage may not be an accurate estimate of the number of eligible families since some military members may be hesitant to enroll family members. Doing so may result in lost assignments or affect promotion rates.[7]

Not surprisingly, my research suggests that military spouses who had children with both special medical and educational needs recorded high stress levels. Specifically, 54.5 percent of military spouses reporting children with special educational needs and 46.6 percent reporting children with medical issues had clinically significant stress levels. These findings suggest that approximately half of military spouses reported clinically significant levels of stress, as compared to spouses without children with special medical or educational needs (27 percent).[1]

Special Child, Special Needs
Ashley's Story

I could tell his brain worked differently from other kids from the age of one. He never looked people in the eye and had a very low attention span. People always told me it was because "he is a boy." This was stressful because in my "mom heart," I knew it was more than "just being a boy." We moved to Okinawa in August of 2014, and my son turned three that September. The move to Okinawa was severely traumatizing for him, which we never expected. His fits were different than what I'd seen other children have, and there weren't many ways to calm him. Prior to moving, we found a preschool in Okinawa to continue the structure and daily routine from his school in America. A week after arriving in Okinawa, he started at that preschool, and I immediately recognized that he was scared, confused, and overwhelmed but unable to express any of those emotions. During this time, I saw things out of him that broke my heart. I remember one night where he cried and screamed for thirty minutes on the curb outside our temporary living facility (TLF). I had another child and groceries to carry up three flights of stairs, but all I could do was sit on the curb next to him until he was ready to move. Our little boy was unable to process or express to me how he felt.

My husband and I eventually found a Montessori-style school with a more open environment, which we thought would suit him better. This was an off-base school in Japan, so we were also dealing with cultural differences. We soon began to receive daily bad behavior reports with my son labeled as a "bully" and a "brat." However, I knew my child was neither. That is when we started to realize that he WAS different and something else was happening.

When he turned four, we went in for his well-child check. We knew this was the point that we were going to ask for our child to be tested for some sort of spectrum disorder or ADHD. His pediatrician was OK with having him tested, but I think he *felt we were reaching for a diagnosis and couldn't accept that this was normal for "just a boy." This is how our journey of having a child with a neurological disorder began, and we quickly realized there was not a clear path for people like us on how to navigate our overseas assignment.*

We were first sent to a behavior specialist at our base medical clinic and then a child screening specialist at one of the on-base schools. Additionally, we had a referral to Mental Health, and we were waiting for them to call so we could schedule an appointment with the base child psychiatrist. I had a child who was clearly struggling, and I was going to different specialists who were doing different tests, all while getting babysitters for a younger child because of a busy husband who was TDY a lot. During this time, we felt we were being sent to places needlessly, and no one knew what to do with us. This was an extremely stressful time in our lives on top of the "normal" military stress we always feel. After waiting months for our first appointment, the wonderful base psychiatrist diagnosed our son within the first ten minutes of our appointment with combined presentation ADHD.

Soon after our son's diagnosis with a neurological disorder, my husband was deployed for a year. I had to navigate how to create the best environment for him and find the best resources in a location with limited options. I had lots of highs and lows that year. One of the highs I'm most thankful for was having a neighbor who also had a child on the spectrum (ADHD and autism), and she became my co-parent that year. This fellow military spouse got me through it. There were times where my son wouldn't get out of the car and would scream and cry because his younger sister got out first. Since disciplining him couldn't be handled quite like other children, situations like these easily escalated to serious meltdowns. I would get my neighbor, and she would simply say, "I got this," and would sit with him for twenty minutes while he screamed. This is the love our military spouses are capable of.

We, luckily, were able to be seen by the same base psychiatrist monthly for almost three years, but when he PCSed, he told us, "If your son's medications do not work as well as they do following my departure, you will probably not be able to stay on the island." His position was not going to have a replacement, so once again, we were in a position where we were worried about our son's medical care.

My son has a neurological disorder that directly impacts his life and well-being as well as our military family. At times, it is extremely frustrating to get him standard specialty care when it is so readily available in the States. As a military spouse, especially one overseas with a child who has special needs, as much as we love the military and love being overseas, I look forward to the day we can make our child's needs a priority without the limitations of an overseas base. We look forward to choosing a home that has access to groups and peer supports with kids more like him.

—Ashley, Air Force Spouse

While all families function with varying degrees of stress, certain stressors among military families may significantly exacerbate such concerns. In this regard, both special education and medical needs of military member's children appear to be two such issues. Children with special needs demand more from a family. These children require more time, attention, and intervention to aid in their physical, mental, emotional, and educational development. As noted by Ashley, the tipping point at which a military family experiences significant clinical levels of stress could be the special needs of their children.

Rational Behavioral Technique 5
Five Rational Questions

A person's behavior springs from his/her ideas.
—Alfred Adler

Restoration is paramount, not only when working through difficult situations but also when learning new ways to think. You will be uncomfortable at times, but real change takes place when you stay patient and stay committed to the process. Let's review where you are within the Emotional Reeducation process.

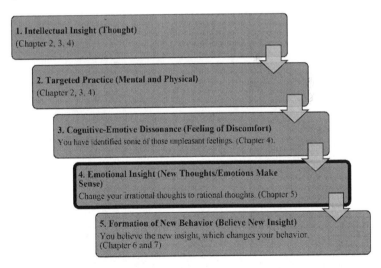

1. **Intellectual Insight (Thought)**
(Chapter 2, 3, 4)

2. **Targeted Practice (Mental and Physical)**
(Chapter 2, 3, 4)

3. **Cognitive-Emotive Dissonance (Feeling of Discomfort)**
You have identified some of those unpleasant feelings. (Chapter 4).

4. **Emotional Insight (New Thoughts/Emotions Make Sense)**
Change your irrational thoughts to rational thoughts. (Chapter 5)

5. **Formation of New Behavior (Believe New Insight)**
You believe the new insight, which changes your behavior. (Chapter 6 and 7)

Emotional insight is when you start to develop new thoughts and understand how they work. We want to change your irrational thoughts to rational thoughts. But what is a rational thought? Rational thoughts and behaviors can be difficult to define. What is rational to you may not be rational to me. For example, in my personal story, what was rational to the military spouse (I was a psychologist and, therefore, had all the answers) was not rational to me. (I had a difficult time with rational thoughts when it came to my son's feelings.) However, according to RBT, rational thoughts do follow five specific criteria.[8]

Five Rules for Optimal Emotional Health

(1) Rational thoughts and behaviors help you habitually feel **SENSITIVELY (S)** the "good" emotions you want to feel (without alcohol or other drugs). No one wants to feel miserable, and rational thoughts help protect you from those unwanted feelings.

Not SENSITIVELY	SENSITIVELY
"Not getting that job makes me a nobody. No one wants me, and I'll never be able to able to work again."	"I didn't get this job, but I'm not going to make myself feel bad. I'm going to start figuring out how to get another job."
The military spouse is beating herself/himself up with bad words.	The military spouse's thoughts will help solve the problem of unemployment/underemployment without making her/him depressed or angry.

(2) Rational thoughts and behaviors help protect your **WELL-BEING (W)**. You want to act on thoughts that will keep you healthy and alive.

Not Good for WELL-BEING	Good for WELL-BEING
"I can't stand it. I will never make it through this deployment. He's better off without me."	"I can stand it because I'm standing it right now. I'm going to stop making myself feel to stop making myself feel bad. I'll calmly change what I can."
The military spouse is thinking thoughts that could lead to self-harm or self-medicating.	The military spouse won't try to self-harm when thinking this way.

(3) Rational thoughts and behaviors help prevent undesirable conflicts/trouble with **OTHERS (O)**. Rational thoughts lead to rational behaviors that ultimately keep you out of conflict.

Leads to Conflict with OTHERS	Prevents Conflict with OTHERS
"I hate the way that woman always flirts with my husband."	"I know she has a tendency to flirt, but I am confident in my relationship with my husband."
The military spouse is thinking thoughts that could lead to conflict.	Even though the military spouse had some concerns, she is rational enough to stay out of conflict.

(4) Rational thoughts and behaviors are based on obvious facts and are **REAL (R)**. It DOES make a difference if you lie to yourself because it makes you feel bad. There is no rational reason to feel bad about the truth. Try using the video camera analogy. Ask yourself: "Would a video camera have recorded the situation exactly as I said it happened?" If the answer is yes, then you probably used facts to describe the situation. However, if the answer is no, then you probably added your opinion about the situation.

Not REAL	REAL
"He always picks his job over me."	"He may have missed some events, but he isn't always gone."
The military spouse isn't thinking rationally and is exaggerating.	The spouse is thinking rationally and is accurate about how it really is.

(5) Rational thoughts and behaviors help achieve both your short- and long-term goals or your **DESTINATION (D)**. Achieving your goals is more likely when your thoughts support success.

Doesn't Lead to Your DESTINATION	Leads to Your DESTINATION
"I want to get a job, but I'm so tired of trying to get a job. No one will hire me. I think I'll stay at home."	"I sure don't feel like getting up and looking for ANOTHER job, but I want the money and the job, so I'll do it."
The military spouse is thinking thoughts that will most likely not support getting a job.	The military spouse is most likely to be successful in finding a job.

Military spouses have to think better before they can feel better, and we know now that we act based on our feelings. Therefore, our behaviors have to be rational too! So, how do you determine if your thoughts and behaviors are rational? You have read the criteria, but let's make it easier to determine rational thoughts and behaviors by changing those criteria into specific questions. Three honest "no" answers reflect irrational thoughts (or behaviors).[9]

(1) Do my thoughts and behaviors help me feel
sensitively? (S)

(2) Do my thoughts and behaviors help me protect my **well-being?** (W)

(3) Do my thoughts and behaviors help me avoid unwanted conflict with **others?** (O)

(4) Are my thoughts and behaviors **real?** (R)

(5) Do my thoughts and behaviors help me reach my **destination?** (D)

Remember:

- What is rational to you may not be rational to others.
- What is rational to you at one particular time may not be rational for you at another time.
- It's unrealistic to meet all five criteria all the time.
- Irrational thoughts and behaviors are those that do not meet at least three of the five criteria at the same time.

Let's make it to remember. As military spouses, we are inundated with acronyms, but alas, they are proven to work. So let's add another one to your list.

SWORD: Five Questions of Rational Behavior

S	• SENSITIVITY
	• Does my behavior help me feel the way I want to?
W	• WELL-BEING
	• Does my behavior help me protect my life and well-being?
O	• OTHERS
	• Does my behavior help me avoid unwanted conflict with others?
R	• REAL
	• Is my behavior based on fact; is it real?
D	• DESTINATION
	• Does my behavior help me achieve my goal or destination?

Figure 17. Lowe, K. 2019. "Five Questions of Rational Behavior: SWORD."
Thrive On, LLC.

As you go through this exercise, use this acronym, SWORD, to help you apply the principles mentioned above to the following scenarios. Much like the Japanese craftsman, as you begin to think about your reactions and evaluate their rational or irrationalness, you begin to fine-tune and hone your SWORD.

Military Spouse Rational vs. Irrational Thoughts

Thoughts and behaviors	Rational	Irrational
"Kellie did not say goodbye the last day before she PCSed. But I'm not going to be upset over her behavior."		
"I just need to get a drink after this horrible week. It's the only thing that will make me feel better."		
Thoughts and behaviors	Rational	Irrational
"I don't know how to do this new job, but I'm going to figure it out. I will not put myself down about not knowing because I can always ask questions."		
"The military really doesn't care about our family."		

Table 7. Lowe, K. 2019. "Application of Rational vs. Irrational Thoughts." Thrive On, LLC.

Thoughts and behaviors	Rational vs. Irrational
"Kellie did not say goodbye the last day before she PCSed. But I'm not going to be upset over her behavior." (RATIONAL)	The military spouse is thinking rationally. She admits not liking what Kellie did but sees there is no point in getting upset when people don't act the way you expect them to. (O) (YES) (OTHERS) Upsetting herself won't change Kellie's behavior, and it won't get her what she wants. (D) (YES) (DESTINA-TION). Additionally, it will just make her feel bad. Since she doesn't want that, she doesn't do it. (S) (YES) (SENSITIVITY)
"I just need a drink after this horrible week. It's the only thing that makes me feel better." (IRRATIONAL)	It's irrational to think you ever need a drink. (R) (NO) (NOT REAL) It is only a strong desire. Your needs are really air, food, water, and shelter. Many times people fool themselves into thinking they "need" a drink when they really just "want" a drink. (W) (NO) (WELL-BEING) you need it, then it is only a matter of of time until you get it. (D) (NO) (Won't lead you to your DESTINATION)
"I don't know how to do this new job, but I'm going to figure it out. I will not put myself down about not knowing because I can always ask questions." (RATIONAL)	This is a very rational thought because the military spouse calmly admits what is unknown. (R) (YES) (REAL) Unlike irrational thoughts of being ignorant or stupid, this military spouse is calmly (S) (YES) (SENSITIVELY) working through the problem to achieve his/her goal. (D) (YES) (DESTINATION)

Thoughts and behaviors	Rational vs. Irrational
"There's no point trying to feel better; the military just doesn't care about our family." **(IRRATIONAL)**	Many people believe they can't feel better. However, people make themselves feel better all the time. (W) (NO) (WELL-BEING) No one feels bad ALL the time. (R) (NO) (NOT REAL) The military spouse stops all the bad feelings as soon as she/he stops thinking the military really doesn't care. (S) (NO) (SENSITIVELY)

Table 7. Lowe, K. 2019. "SWORD Applied to Rational vs. Irrational Thoughts."
Thrive On, LLC.

By continually evaluating your thoughts and behaviors, you will begin to naturally notice when they are rational and irrational. You will hone your responses and strengthen your mindset. It is not easy and takes continual practice; that is why the five questions were developed to give you concrete tools. As military spouses, it is imperative that we take time to restore ourselves after our setbacks. Irrational thoughts and behaviors can certainly arise after setbacks because of the additional stress that forced us into the restoration stage. It is because of military spouses, such as those presented thus far, that I have compiled the following exercises, in hopes they will provide a way to a less stress-filled place.

Reflection Questions

(1) Why do you think it is important to have a stage for spouses called "restoration"?

_____

_____

_____

_____

_____

_____

_____

(2) Have you ever wished that you were unbreakable? Why or why not?

_____

_____

_____

_____

_____

_____

_____

(3) Look back on your description of the "stressed spouse." Was your description accurate? Were you surprised by the demographic results?

_____

_____

_____

_____

_____

_____

_____

(4) Do you believe you are currently in the restoration stage? If yes, how long have you been in this stage? If no, recall a time that you believe you were in this stage and describe it below.

_____

_____

_____

_____

_____

_____

_____

(5) Write down your thoughts and behaviors during your time in the restoration stage.

Thoughts	Behaviors

(6) Look at your responses and ask yourself the five questions.

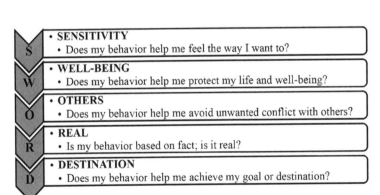

- **SENSITIVITY**
  - Does my behavior help me feel the way I want to?
- **WELL-BEING**
  - Does my behavior help me protect my life and well-being?
- **OTHERS**
  - Does my behavior help me avoid unwanted conflict with others?
- **REAL**
  - Is my behavior based on fact; is it real?
- **DESTINATION**
  - Does my behavior help me achieve my goal or destination?

(7) Circle your rational thoughts and behaviors; put an
X through the irrational thoughts and behaviors.
(*** Remember: it has to meet three of the five questions.)

_____

_____

_____

_____

_____

_____

_____

_____

(8) Share with a family member, or with your group, or
write below why you believe you had the thoughts and
behaviors that you wrote down.

_____

_____

_____

_____

_____

_____

_____

_____

Exercises

(1) Label the following statements. Put an "F" if they are facts or an "O" if they are opinions.

    _____   I can't do anything right.

    _____   All my spouse does is criticize everything I do.

    _____   I was late for work three times this week.

    _____   Captain Jones is a jerk for sending my spouse on another TDY.

    _____   Lauren lies about everything.

    _____   Yesterday, Lauren lied about going to the BX.

(2) Apply the "camera check" to these situations. (Ask yourself: "Would a video camera have recorded the situation exactly as I said it happened?") Write down the facts and only the facts!

I stayed up late last night binge-watching Netflix and had to have a snack. I ate constantly all night.

_____

_____

_____

_____

_____

_____

The children were driving me crazy last night. They wouldn't go to bed until all hours of the night.

_____

_____

_____

_____

_____

_____

My husband and I went to the commissary with the kids. He rudely ignored me when I asked him to check how busy the line was inside the commissary. (It was payday, after all.)

_____

_____

_____

_____

_____

_____

My spouse treated me like crap because I forgot my military ID at home. She said I was irresponsible and disorganized.

_____

_____

_____

_____

_____

_____

(3) Label the following statements. Put an "R" if they are rational thoughts and behaviors or an "I" if they are irrational thoughts and behaviors. Remember the five questions.

- **SENSITIVITY**
  - Does my behavior help me feel the way I want to?
- **WELL-BEING**
  - Does my behavior help me protect my life and well-being?
- **OTHERS**
  - Does my behavior help me avoid unwanted conflict with others?
- **REAL**
  - Is my behavior based on fact; is it real?
- **DESTINATION**
  - Does my behavior help me achieve my goal or destination?

_____ There's no use trying to feel better.

_____ My spouse didn't come home on time last Friday night, and I didn't like it.

_____ I can't stand to be criticized.

_____ My spouses's commander has no place telling me
where I can or cannot work.

_____ I'm disappointed that my spouse has to deploy,
and I'm going to tell him or her.

_____ I control myself; I cannot control anyone else.

Sources

1. Lowe, K. 2016. "5 Ways to Manage Military Spouse Stress."
Military Spouse Magazine, 12 (8).

2. Kudler, H., and Porter, R. 2013. "Building Communities of
Care for Military Families and Children." *Future of Children*, 23,
163–185.

3. Solomon, Z. (1993). *Combat Stress Reaction: The Enduring Toll
of War*. Plenum Publishing Corporation: New York.

4. Storm, T., Gavian, M., Possis, E., Loughlin, J., Bui, T., Linardatos,
E., Leskela, J., and Siegel, W. 2012. "Cultural and Ethical Consid-
erations When Working with Military Personnel and Veterans: A
Primer for VA Training Programs." *Training and Education In
Professional Psychology*, 6, 67–75.

5. Defense Primer: Exceptional Family Member Program (EFMP)
2018. Retrieved from https://fas.org.sgp/crs/natsec/IF11049.pdf.

6. Military One Source. 2019. "EFMP/Special Needs." Retrieved
from https://www.militaryonesource.mil/family-relationships/
special-needs/exceptional-family-member/the-exceptional-family-
member-program-for-families-with-special-needs.

7. Maxwell, N. 2013. "EFMP is Positive for Families Not Negative
for Careers." US Army. Retrieved from http://www.army.mil/
article/110436/EFMP_is_positive_not_negative_for_careers/

8. Maultsby, M.C. 1990. *Rational Behavioral Therapy*. Rational Self-Help Aids: Wisconsin.

9. Maultsby, M. C. and Hendricks, M.A. 1974. *You and Your Emotions*. Self-Help Books Divisions: Kentucky.

6

Strengthen
If You Want It, Work For It

Life is a grindstone. Whether it grinds us down or polishes us up depends on us.
—Thomas L. Holdcroft

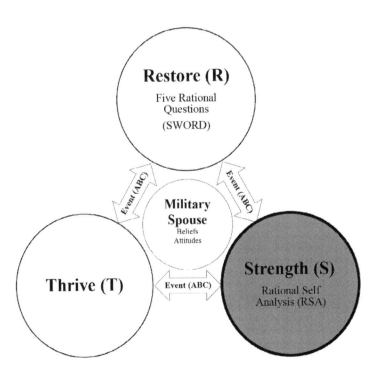

Strengthen

Congratulations, you have worked hard to get here, and now it is time to strengthen your skills. Just as Japanese sword-smiths use forged heat to give a sword strength and a sharp edge, the skills learned during this stage provide the strength necessary to not only absorb setbacks but also to enable you to move forward after disappointments. The truth is military spouses can support each other. We utilize our collective strength by reinforcing individual self-help skills that move us all toward improved emotional health. The concepts presented in this chapter are designed to reinforce what has already been discussed and make you stronger. As noted in previous chapters, learning to think, feel, and act rationally takes practice. Be patient with yourself. When you allow yourself sufficient time and put forth a consistent effort, you will be rewarded with a time when you begin to think, feel, and act in a much more self-satisfying manner.

My Experience

It's hard for me to reach out when I am struggling. I find it virtually impossible to focus on building my coping skills when I am literally on the brink of tears, when I want to scream or just crawl into bed. However, I have learned the value of waiting until I am emotionally stronger to gain new skills. I can listen more intently, accept new ideas, and try them out when I am NOT distracted by significant setbacks.

About our third year into our assignment in North Carolina, I found myself just a little bit stronger. I was coming to terms with the four-month rotational deployment and had crafted a way to balance our new, chaotic, unstructured normal. I was ready to step a little out of my comfort zone, so when one of my closest friends, Trish, invited me to a group called Wives of Warriors (WOW), I accepted. Reflecting back, I know that if I were in a different stage of my life as a military spouse, I would have passed, primarily because the thought of immersing myself in a fishbowl with other military spouses was distressing (or so I thought). With a little encouragement, I decided to go to my first meeting.

We gathered in a small community center where the mentors of the group provided refreshments for all the military spouses on an early Friday morning. Church volunteers also provided childcare for the military spouses so we could attend the meeting. This was a gift in itself. The chairs were all aligned facing the front of the room, where a podium stood on a stage. I assumed it was prepped for the pastor who was going to preach his message to us. I was so wrong.

The room quieted down and the founder of WOW walked onto the stage. She reminded us of the importance of confidentially in our group (think group counseling) and then introduced Roger Watson. I was curious how this man was going to fit into this private circle of military spouses. Roger spoke—and I was riveted.

Transcript of Roger's Testimony to the Wives of Warriors (WOW), Offered in October 2014

Being in the military, working out is part of our routine. On April 26, 2016, I was at the gym doing my cardio and weights, and as I went upstairs, I thought, "Gee, I'm not feeling good." I was going to leave and go to the truck and go home, but I didn't. I went upstairs and lay down on a mat with a foam roller on my spine, which I usually do at the end of a workout to stretch. That's when I went quietly to "the other side." I was dead for two and a half minutes.

I had a 95 percent blockage in two major arteries. My brain was not getting any oxygen, and my heart went into ventricular fibrillation (VFib). The AED brought my heart back to a normal rhythm, and I was transported to the hospital, where they installed two stents.

If what I experienced was death, I am ready for it. It's the most peaceful feeling I ever had in my life. What all this taught me is not to fear death. It may sound funny to say this, especially after all the years doing what I did in the military. But if that is what it's like, I have no problem with it.

Today, there's nothing different about me as a human. I'm like many of your husbands. I grew up in the military and as a Christian. My brother and I lived all over the world as kids: Germany, Japan, and many places in the US. I spent my childhood playing baseball, and when I wasn't playing ball, I was in church or scouting. I grew up like a normal kid. After high school, I went to college and in a short time realized it was not for me and dropped out. All I wanted to do was play ball and work to make enough money to date beautiful women. It didn't take me very long to find out that wasn't going to work, so I joined the military.

I did some careful reflection about my life after this event, which was a wake-up call. I've looked back at things that happened to me, and I'm convinced that this was not the only occasion that God intervened. God gave me the skill and training as a solider to stay alive. When that didn't work, he stepped in. I can think of so many incidents in Vietnam—in '65, '66, '67, and '68—the firefights where people stepped in front of me and took a bullet and lived, but it could have been me. I think how I was seconds away from SKUD attacks in the first Gulf War. I think about my most recent experience in Pakistan, where I had just left the hotel I'd been living in for weeks when it was bombed—destroying it and killing so many. I didn't think of any of this until this [SCA] happened.

I realized God had something more in mind for me. I am a good Christian, and my wife and I try hard to live by the standard every day. But we also know we can always ask for HIS forgiveness and will be forgiven.

I finished my career this summer (2014) after fifty years of service, and now I'm going to try and be a better husband, a better Christian, and a better father. Thank you all for your service and God bless you.

—Roger Watson, LTC, Special Forces, Retired

During the presentation, Roger and his wife, Claudia, offered to help the WOW group. Following this event, for the first time, I reached out for help. They scheduled monthly visits to my house to help with outside chores, as I was yet to figure out how to mow the lawn with three babies. An initial attempt with my son strapped to my chest in a baby carrier and the girls corralled on the screened-in porch resulted in a pool of frustration. Within minutes, my son blew out his diaper, and as I walked inside to change both of our outfits, I noticed the girls had managed to climb into the house via the doggy door—funny at first, until I discovered they had taken the sidewalk chalk inside with them and drawn pictures on the INSIDE walls with the OUTSIDE chalk. The lawn did NOT get mowed that day.

Roger and Claudia scheduled monthly visits and, upon their arrival, would promptly tell me to go inside and nap with the kids, and I did just that.

A year later, Roger passed from an unexpected heart attack, and as I sat with Claudia the day before his funeral, I told her how grateful I was for their help in the past year. Her response shocked me. Her voice trembled as she expressed, "You have it wrong, Kendra. You gave Roger the greatest gift by allowing us to help. Since his retirement, he still wanted to serve and help our military families. You gave him that opportunity, and that meant the world to him. It is you who I should be thanking." I was speechless. I had no idea that reinforcing my skill of accepting help and resources would not only improve my life but have a profound effect on others.

Roger Watson, LTC, Special Forces, served two more years—a total of fifty-two years of service to his country. He was scheduled to deploy for an overseas assignment the week following Christmas but died very suddenly on December 26, 2014, at home with his wife, Claudia. His last words to her as she kissed him and raced for the EMS team, "Babe, I love you."

Learned Resourcefulness

Military spouses can bounce back after repeated setbacks. In fact, they are very good at bouncing back because we are forced to do it so often. Running away from stress isn't an option because stress is around every corner. When we have no way of avoiding stress, we can learn from it.

I've met many military spouses who have learned successful strategies to handle stress. Psychologists use the term "learned resourcefulness."[1] Learned resourcefulness is different than resiliency. Learned resourcefulness refers to what we are capable of as military spouses, whereas resiliency refers to our ability to recover from stressful situations.

To explain further, in 2015, RAND Corporation conducted a study to help the Air Force better understand military resiliency. One theme they identified is that resiliency can only be measured in the context of stress.[2] In my opinion, military spouses need to build and grow despite the stressful event. Learned resourcefulness is a better representation of what we are capable of as military spouses. As previously mentioned, it is the ability to reach out for help during deployment and to find your tribe at a new PCS location. It is connecting with a new military family life counselor (MFLC) to help you work on your own emotional health. Learned resourcefulness is what every military spouse needs to know how to do, not just to survive but to thrive.

Resiliency is a measure of how we respond to personal stress. What follows is the Brief Resiliency Scale created by Bruce Smith and colleagues in 2008. This scale was specifically developed to measure an individual's ability to "bounce back from stress."[3]

Brief Resiliency Scale

Mark ONE box per row	Strongly Disagree	Disagree	Neutral	Agree	Strongly Agree
I tend to bounce back quickly after hard times.	1	2	3	4	5
I have a hard time making it through stressful events.	5	4	3	2	1
It does not take me long to recover from stressful events.	1	2	3	4	5
It is hard for me to snap back when something happens.	5	4	3	2	1
I usually come through difficult times with little trouble.	1	2	3	4	5
I tend to take a long time to get over setbacks in my life.	5	4	3	2	1

Figure 18. Brief Resiliency Scale. Smith, B.W., Dalan, J., Wiggins, K., Tooley, E., Christopher, P., and Bernard, J. (2008). The brief resilience scale: assessing the ability to bounce back. *International Journal of Behavioral Medicine*, 15(3), 194–200.

Scoring: Add the responses varying from 1–5 for all six items giving a range from 6–30. Then divide your answer by 6.

_____Total score

_____Total Score divided by 6

BRS Score	Classification
1.0–2.99	Low Resilience
3.0–4.3	Normal Resilience
4.31–5.0	High Resilience

Were you surprised by your score? If yes, the good news is you can make the choice to change your score. If not, then I would propose you still have room to grow by learning how to maximize your resourcefulness! So let's begin.

Available Resources

Have you heard the term post-traumatic growth? It is a term that is becoming more and more common today. It is the ability to grow after a personal tragedy, as opposed to struggling (post-traumatic stress disorder). Sheryl Sandberg, in her book *Option B*, expertly combines stories of adversity, resiliency, and joy to reflect post-traumatic growth. After reading this book several times, I believe its basic premise is applicable to the lives of military spouses.

I know, you are thinking, "Do I really need to go through a personal tragedy in the military just to be able to grow? Luckily, the answer is no. Learning resourcefulness is developing what psychologists now call pre-traumatic stress growth.[4] It's building up a social-emotional barrier for whatever lies ahead. This barrier is what we need as military spouses. The reality is life is full of stressful events, especially military life. And then there are tragic events. The military provides many resources for stressful as well as tragic events at many different levels.

Special Level Resources

There are many forms of support designed to ensure military family stability. Since 9/11, numerous programs aimed at meeting the needs of contemporary military families have been developed. These programs take place at various levels, including special military commands, military communities, and the Department of Defense. One program implemented by the United States Special Operations Command is called Preservation of the Force and Family (POTFF).[5] The mission of the POTFF initiative is "to identify and implement innovative, valuable solutions ... aimed at improving the short and long-term well-being of our Special Operations Forces (SOF) warriors and their families."[5]

I attended a POTFF-funded program while in North Carolina. It provided a weekend retreat, complete with childcare and chaplain services, to help with the reintegration process after my husband's return from a long deployment. I found myself depressed postdeployment and thought I was crazy for it. Who wouldn't be thrilled to have their husband home? But I realized that weekend that I was dealing with so much more than just the deployment.

—Sarah, Air Force Spouse

Another initiative called Families Overcoming Under Stress (FOCUS) was created by the University of California, Los Angeles (UCLA) and the Harvard School of Medicine. This prevention program was specially developed for military families at Camp Pendleton. It teaches families how to cope with separation, routine shifts, and fear of loss of the active-duty member, as well as the physical and psychological stress experienced by active-duty members. This comprehensive program was developed to teach resiliency skills to active-duty members, dependent spouses, and their children.[6]

My husband has been a Marine for fifteen years—I wondered what they could possibly tell me that I don't already know. I was surprised by all the information we actually used.

—FOCUS Mom, Marine Corps Spouse

Since 2008, FOCUS has expanded and now serves thirty Navy, Marine, Air Force, and Army bases, supporting approximately 743,000 military families. While at Kadena Air Base as a school psychologist, I was able to work closely with this program. I often made referrals to FOCUS when I encountered military families that were struggling and personally witnessed the tremendous positive impact the program has on military families.

National-Level Resources

At the national level, communities have developed several associations, such as the National Military Family Association (NMFA) and the Military Child Education Coalition (MCEC), aimed at supporting military families.[6] Even the professional psychology association has taken notice. The American Psychological Association (APA) developed the Task Force on Military Deployment Services for Youth, Families, and Service Members. This APA program is aimed at helping professional psychologists recognize and respond to the unique needs of military families.[7]

In 2009, the Department of Defense instituted a program called Coming Together Around Military Families (CTAMF). This program provides professional training, consultations, and materials to military families in over sixty-five communities.[8]

The Department of Defense has also emphasized the challenges associated with reintegration and initiated a program called Strong Families. This home-based parenting program contains eight intervention modules designed to help military families during critical time periods. Strong Families pays increased attention to deployment stress (child separation and active-duty member mental health problems), parent-child relationships, and parenting and parenting stress during reintegration that, as reflected in the previous chapter on perseverance, is critical within our community. It is reported that 90 percent of military families who enter will finish the program.[9]

A recently initiated program aimed at meeting the needs of military families is the Military and Family Life Counseling Program (MFLC). The MFLC Program trains consultants to counsel military families on relationships, crisis intervention, stress management, grief, occupational, and other special and family-related issues.[10] This program, unlike other military support programs, provides a Child and Youth Program (CYP), which is integrated into school systems to explicitly help military children.

I have personally worked with some amazing MFLC professionals, both in the school system at Kadena and my husband's operations group. These trained professionals work tirelessly to help our military families. If you don't know who your MFLC is, ask! They are often embedded into squadrons for quick and easy access. As told by Michelle, we have military spouses and children who reap the benefits of our MFLCs all the time.

Can I Keep My MFLC?
Michelle's Story

I was so excited to finally find a counselor who I liked! My friend had recently recommended a new MFLC assigned to our husband's group, and she told me she really liked her, so I thought I would give it a try. I was skeptical at first because I had gone to counselors before and just didn't make a connection. Well, maybe that's not completely true. I did find one who was amazing three years ago, but then we had to move. And I didn't make the effort to find another one—probably because I thought I didn't need one anymore.

But three years later, I found myself struggling with the same issues. I didn't feel like I had an identity in the Army separate from my husband, and I wanted to find a way to be, well, happier with myself. So I was excited to get a personal recommendation of a counselor who worked well with military spouses—not to mention I knew MFLCs did not take notes, and there was a certain comfort that came with that fact. I called to schedule my first meeting, and she actually recommended we meet for coffee for the first time to get to know each other. I didn't know that MFLCs could meet with spouses outside their offices. We hit it off immediately.

I saw the MFLC weekly for two months and was making REAL progress. We had developed a personal goal for myself: to work on building my photography business, and we mapped out clear details to get there. I was feeling probably the strongest I ever had as a military spouse. And then it hit. She told me it was time for her to rotate to a new base. I was devastated. I didn't know if I could finish what we started alone. I needed her. Later, I reminded myself of all that I had gained by working with her, but I have to be honest. It left a hole for quite a while.

—Michelle, Army Spouse

Military Spouses as a Collective Resource

We are often our own best resource! In fact, researchers have found repeatedly that social support is one of the strongest tools designed to help military families. We become stronger together because we have common experiences. When we share our stories with those around us, we connect. That connection helps us from feeling so alone and isolated. For example, when one spouse shares the struggle of finding a good school in a new area, there are most likely others who relate, and then a connection, a community, is created.

> We don't need love and belonging and story-catching from everyone in our lives, but we need it from at least one person—if we have a friend, or small group of friends, or family who embraces our imperfections, vulnerabilities, and power, and fills us with a sense of belonging, we are incredibly lucky.[11]
>
> —Brené Brown, *The Gift of Imperfection*

We Are Stronger Together
Crystal's Story

Your desire to stay a military spouse will be tested often, but nothing quite compares to the death of a friend. For me, that day came on February 18, 2007, when my husband walked into our bedroom holding our two-week-old daughter and told me that his, our, closest friend had passed away in a helicopter crash four days after he walked out of our front door. My world literally came to a standstill. Not only was my husband broken into a million little pieces, but our now deceased friend had a family that we had to help notify with Air Force officials. His widow was my best friend; his family was our family. How does one even begin to start this process? Do I get all the screaming and crying out first? Impossible. It lasted for months—years— after. In the days, months, and years that followed, we learned to dig as deeply as possible to support whomever, wherever, or whenever someone needed it. It was actually shocking (and somewhat rewarding)—just how much people leaned on US for support. We had just lost OUR best friend, but we found ourselves in this stressful role of constant support and guidance, from making funeral arrangements to reading his autopsy report; it was almost unbearable.

After the dust settled, we had to figure out how to move on with a large part of our "family" missing. When I say "we," I mean "me." My husband, who happened to do the same job as our friend, was about to deploy. I had a distraught eight-year-old son traumatized by his pseudo-dad's death, a two-year-old, and a newborn baby girl. Every part of my body and soul hurt. I spent every single day with his widow and their baby girl, who was only four months old at the time of his death. We cried. We laughed. We were silent. We tried to be normal. We had huge fights. I was unsure of almost everything, except for one thing. I was completely lost and just wanted our friend to call me and tell me what to do.

Most days, all I wanted was a "normal" life—one that didn't involve war and death. I wanted to walk away and pretend like this life never existed. Prior to yet another deployment that I quite frankly could not believe the Air Force was making my husband do, I asked him: "Why are you doing this? Why do you WANT to keep doing your job? You can die! For what! What the hell did he die for? Why leave us?"

He stopped in his tracks and said, "Honey, there are very bad people in this world who want to do very bad things to you—to our kids—to Americans at large. The ONLY thing standing between people like them and you—is people like me."

Two things happened at that moment. I knew he spoke the truth, and I had to accept that deploying was part of the job. I also needed to dig deeply, make a choice, and turn this life-changing event into something good. HE would have wanted that. So I got involved. I got involved with the Gold Star Family events. We did Wreaths Across America yearly. We supported his family in whatever way that meant. We started a memorial box for his daughter to be opened when she is eighteen, and fill it, to this day, with everything left at his grave for her to open so she can know how much he was loved. Memorial Day and Veterans Day took on a whole new meaning. We participate in Memorial runs. We sit on the lawn of the Nation's Capital, and we remember.

More importantly, for me, as a military spouse, this horrible event made me understand the "why" in our military family.

I was given a lot of resources and helpful tips during the grief process that I can share as a key spouse mentor to help my younger spouses. To this day, I still reach back to the painful memories of losing our friend and talk about the lessons learned so that they may help others. The most valuable lesson being— lean on each other as military spouses and ask for help. I know it's not easy to ask for help, but we must ask for help and give help freely because we can be stronger together.

—Crystal Cox, Air Force Spouse

As Crystal's painful story illustrates, military families are their own best resource. We are fortunate to have many resources that our very own military spouses have developed to help our community. For example, InDependent, Incorporated was founded in 2013 by five military spouses who identified a need in our military community for a social wellness program. This nonprofit organization hosts an annual Military Spouse Wellness Summit (attended by over 4,600 military spouses)! Each year, a different theme is presented to help military spouses. This program also provides an online wellness lounge for spouses and related events aimed at promoting healthy lifestyles.[12]

BOOST Leadership, founded by military spouses Cassandra Martinez and Betsy Eves, provides a day training on the tools and mindset needed to increase leadership and management skills among military spouses. A major goal of BOOST is to help military spouses stay on a path of constant growth.[13]

Military spouse Corie Weathers provides counseling to help military families grow in their marriage, parenting, and/or effectiveness in serving military and first responder families. The program, Lifegiver, highlights her expertise as a military clinical consultant.[14] Richelle Futch wrote the book *Her Ruck* to address the emotional backpacks we carry as military spouses.[15] 2017 Military Spouse of the Year, Brittany Boccher, along with military spouse Molly Bennett, created Discovering Your Spark, which coaches military spouses how to better define their purpose and passion.[16]

While this list is by no means exhaustive, it highlights available resources and some amazing spouses! However, despite such resources, one question remains: why do many of these resources continue to be underutilized? The answer is because many of these resources require military spouses to step outside their comfort zones. Since such resources may not be available in every location, individuals may need to help themselves by using tools designed to guide them through the process of rational thinking.

One such learned resourcefulness tool you can use to help yourself to better emotional health is called rational self-analysis (RSA).

Rational Behavioral Technique 6
Rational Self-Analysis

> *You are not what you think you are,*
> *but what you think you are.*
> —Norman Vincent Peale

RSA is a quick way to get into a self-help activity, right now. This book has introduced you to a lot of new ideas, and you may be thinking, "OK, I accept I create my own emotions, and

I probably think irrationally sometimes, and this makes me feel ways I don't want to feel, but what can I do to address more challenging situations?" RSA is a tool designed to address such problems. This technique is designed to help you understand and, if needed, change problematic thoughts, feelings, and actions. The good news is RSA utilizes the information already discussed in this book. Now it is time to put all the concepts we have learned into practice—we all learn best by doing.[17]

RSA Checklist

		Process	Letter
	1.	Separate the event into your ABCs.	(A) (Facts) (B) (Thoughts) (C) (Feelings)
	2.	Write down new facts about (A) if they need to be corrected.	(Da) (Camera check)
	3.	Write rational statements to substitute irrational thoughts. (SWORD)	(Db) (SWORD)
	4.	Write down the way you want to feel.	(E1)
	5.	Write down how you acted and how you want to act in the future.	(C2) (E2)

Table 8. Adapted from Maultsby, M. C. and Hendricks, M.A. 1974. *You and Your Emotions.* Self-Help Books Divisions: Kentucky.

Rational Self-Analysis Template

A. FACTS and EVENTS:	Da. CAMERA CHECK:
List only the facts — in simple terms.	If you put anything in (A) section that is not factual, correct it here. **Remember it is as if you a video camera has recorded the events.
B. SELF TALK:	**Db. CHALLENGE & ALTERNATIVES**
Write down all the thoughts you had while in the event or about the event in (A). (B1) (B2) (B3)	Challenge each thought (B), according to the five questions (SWORD). (D1) (D2) (D3)
C1. FEELINGS:	**E1. DESIRED FEELINGS:**
Statement of your feelings about (A). ("I felt angry" or "I felt depressed.")	Statement describing how you want to feel in the future about this situation.
C2. ACTIONS:	**E2. DESIRED ACTION**
Write down what you did.	Write down what you wish you had done.

- **SENSITIVITY**
  - Does my behavior help me feel the way I want to?
- **WELL-BEING**
  - Does my behavior help me protect my life and well-being?
- **OTHERS**
  - Does my behavior help me avoid unwanted conflict with others?
- **REAL**
  - Is my behavior based on fact; is it real?
- **DESTINATION**
  - Does my behavior help me achieve my goal or destination?

Figure 19. Adapted from Maultsby, M. C. and Hendricks, M.A. 1974. *You and Your Emotions.* Self-Help Books Divisions: Kentucky.

RSA Military Spouse Application

A. FACTS and EVENTS:	Da. CAMERA CHECK:
The military made a bad call (subject); they are making us move after eighteen months instead of the promised three years.	My husband's boss just called and informed him that we have to move to Florida in March.
B. SELF TALK:	**Db. CHALLENGE & ALTERNATIVES**
(B1) My husband's boss is an idiot.	(D1) He is an "idiot" in an untrue statement. It's not based on fact. (**R: not real**) It's an organization that can make quick decisions that are frustrating. (**S: it is not making me feel the way I want to feel.**) (**W: it did not protect my well-being.**)
(B2) They are playing favorites to other people in the squadron because I know they have granted assignment extensions.	(D2) I don't know that they are playing favorites and assuming this is only making me upset. (**R: not real**) (**S: not making me feel the way I want to feel.**) (**O: it is not helping me avoid conflict with others.**)
(B3) It's unfair; they never consider our family's needs and wants.	(D3) What's fair is not a relevant issue. (**O: it is not helping me avoid unwanted conflict with others**) What they did is not illegal. We have to move because it is what his job requires. (**D: it did not help achieve goals/destination**) (**S: it did not help me feel the way I want to**).
C1. FEELINGS:	**E1. DESIRED FEELINGS:**
Anger, hostility	Calm disappointment about not being able to stay in the current location.
C2. ACTIONS:	**E2. DESIRED ACTION**
Scream at my husband and work myself up over the pending move.	Do not scream at my husband. Calmly discuss the news with family or friends.

Figure 20. Lowe, K. 2019. "Military Spouse Rational Self-Analysis." Thrive On, LLC.

In this example, the military spouse is clearly frustrated with a short-notice PCS, and her thoughts reflect her anger. Her three main thoughts were irrational for the following reasons:

(1) "My husband's boss is an idiot." First, the statement is not real (**R**), it is based on her opinion. Second, the comment did not make her feel the way she wanted to feel (**S**) because she became angry and hostile. She was not thinking of her well-being because it could cause future problems with her husband's boss (**W**). Finally, it caused conflict with her husband (**O**).

(2) "They are playing favorites with other people in the squadron because I know they have granted assignment extensions." This also did not pass the rational thought questions. The belief that the squadron is playing favorites is not real; it is another opinion (**R**). The statement did not make her feel the way she wanted to (**S**). It could cause further conflict with spouses if she believes there are favorites in the squadron (**O**).

(3) "It's unfair; they never consider our family's needs and wants." Struggling with fairness led to conflict with others because she yelled at her husband about having to move (**O**). Arguing the military's decision goes against their family goal or destination to provide for their family (**D**). Again, it led to negative emotions about the military in general (**S**).

It takes time and practice to effectively work through an RSA, but you CAN do it. An RSA can be applied to positive, negative, and neutral emotions. Try to do one a day for the next week. Pick an event, any event, and work through the RSA (see exercises).

The strengthening stage is a specific time to embrace learned resourcefulness. Each time you cycle through this stage, you can get stronger, faster, and leaner by maximizing your ability to help yourself.

Reflection Questions

(1) Recall a time you were in the strengthening stage. Describe that time below.

_____

_____

_____

_____

_____

_____

_____

(2) Do you think you have mastered learned resourcefulness? Why or why not?

_____

_____

_____

_____

_____

_____

_____

(3) Have you utilized any of the resources mentioned in this chapter? Which ones did you like? Not like? Why?

_____

_____

_____

_____

_____

_____

_____

(4) Share with a friend (or your group) some resources that are not mentioned in this chapter. Describe the strengths and weaknesses of that resource.

_____

_____

_____

_____

_____

_____

_____

(5) What was your reaction to the term "pre-traumatic growth?" Do you believe this is attainable? Why or why not?

_____

_____

_____

_____

_____

_____

_____

_____

_____

_____

Exercises

(1) Go to the "Resources" section of this chapter and pick one resource that you want to learn more about or that interests you. You don't have to sign up for or attend anything, just start exploring!

(2) Conduct one RSA per day for seven days. Pick any event during that day (positive, negative, or neutral). Then use the RSA form below. (Go over it with a friend or with your group.)

A. FACTS and EVENTS:	Da. CAMERA CHECK:
List only the facts — in simple terms.	If you put anything in (A) section that is not factual, correct it here. **Remember it is as if you a video camera has recorded the events.
B. SELF TALK:	**Db. CHALLENGE & ALTERNATIVES**
Write down all the thoughts you had while in the event or about the event in (A).	Challenge each thought (B), according to the five questions (SWORD).
(B1) (B2) (B3)	(D1) (D2) (D3)
C1. FEELINGS:	**E1. DESIRED FEELINGS:**
Statement of your feelings about (A). ("I felt angry" or "I felt depressed.")	Statement describing how you want to feel in the future about this situation.
C2. ACTIONS:	**E2. DESIRED ACTION**
Write down what you did.	Write down what you wish you had done.

- **SENSITIVITY**
  - Does my behavior help me feel the way I want to?
- **WELL-BEING**
  - Does my behavior help me protect my life and well-being?
- **OTHERS**
  - Does my behavior help me avoid unwanted conflict with others?
- **REAL**
  - Is my behavior based on fact; is it real?
- **DESTINATION**
  - Does my behavior help me achieve my goal or destination?

(3) Start a "feel good" file, journal, or scrapbook. Print out emails, text messages, cards, and private messages that people have sent to you. Gather these items often, and make sure you print them out and they are not just stored in the cloud. When you find yourself having a rough day, pull out this folder. Read through some of the items. Even if the person who wrote to you is not a significant part of your life anymore, the words can help uplift you on a particularly stressful day.

Sources

1. Antonovsky, A. 1990. "Pathways to Leading to Successful Coping and Health." In M. Rosenbaum (Ed.). *Learned Resourcefulness: On Coping Skills, Self-Control, and Adaptive Behavior*, 31–63. New York: Springer-Verlag.

2. Meadows, S. O., Miller, L. L., and Robson, S. 2015. *Airman and Family Resilience: Lessons from the Scientific Literature.* Santa Monica: RAND Corporation.

3. Smith, B.W., Dalan, J., Wiggins, K., Tooley, E., Christopher, P., and Bernard, J. 2008. "The Brief Resilience Scale: Assessing the Ability to Bounce Back." *International Journal of Behavioral Medicine*, 15(3), 194–200.

4. Sandberg, S. and Grant, A. 2017. *Option B: Facing Adversity, Building Resiliency, and Finding Joy.* New York: Alfred A. Knopf.

5. United States Special Operations Command (USSOCOM) 2019. "Preservation of the Force and Family." Retrieved from https://www.socom.mil/POTFF/Pages/default.aspx

6. Kudler, H., and Porter, R. 2013. "Building Communities of Care for Military Families and Children." *Future of Children*, 23, 163–185.

7. American Psychological Association Presidential Task Force on Military Deployment Services for Youth Families and Service Members. 2007. "The Psychological Needs of US Military Service Members and Their Families: A Preliminary Report." Washington, DC: American Psychological Association.

8. Osofsky, J. D. and Chartrand, M.M. 2013. "Military Children from Birth to Five Years." *Future of Children*, 23, 61–77.

9. Ross, A., and DeVoe, E. 2014. "Engaging Military Parents in Home-Based Reintegration Program: A Consideration of Strategies." *Health and Social Work*. 39, 47–54.

10. MHN Government Services 2019. "Military and Family Life Counseling (MFLC) Program." Retrieved from www.mhngs.com/app/programsandservices/mf-lc_program.content

11. Brown, B. 2010. *The Gifts of Imperfection: Let Go of Who You Think You're Supposed to be and Embrace Who you Are*. Minnesota: Hazelden Publishing.

12. InDependent, Incorporated 2019. Retrieved from https://in-dependent.org/about.

13. Boost Leadership Accelerator 2018. Retrieved from http://boostleader.com/about/.

14. Lifegiver Clinician Directory 2019. Retrieved from https://www.life-giver.org/

15. Futch, R. 2018. *Her Ruck: Inside the Emotional Backpack of Military Wives*. Richelle Futch, MSW.

16. Bushatz, A. 2018. "This Awesome Workbook Will Help You Find Your Purpose." Retrieved from https://www.military.com/spousebuzz/2018/05/21/awesome-workbook-will-help-you-find-your-purpose.html

17. Maultsby, M. C. and Hendricks, M.A. 1974. *You and Your Emotions*. Self-Help Books Divisions: Kentucky.

7

Thrive On
Be the Hero of Your Own Story

Life is either a daring adventure or nothing. To keep our
faces toward change and behave like free spirits in the
presence of fate is strength undefeatable.
—Helen Keller

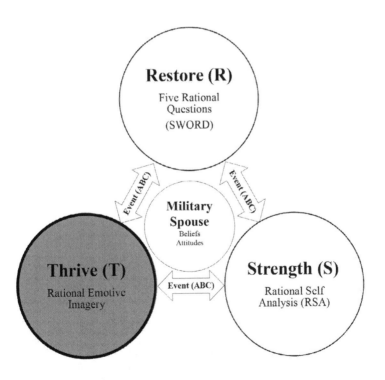

Thrive On

Thriving is the final life cycle stage where military spouses embrace a moment of personal success, a triumph, or a victory over the constant setbacks. This stage can be reflected by your family's success in completing a 5K, a promotion at work, a son's acceptance into college, finding a new church that fits your family, or being emotionally stronger by overcoming depressive thoughts. These are all common examples of when people free themselves from irrational thoughts, feelings, and actions. Thriving is a time in which we set and accomplish goals that may have been long overdue. As the swordsmith grinds a blade to a precise edge, the military spouse's ability to thrive is sharpened through prescribed stages of social-emotional development. Remember that this stage, like all the previous stages, is not a stationary stage but is a constantly changing state. Choosing to thrive despite stressful conditions will bring comfort and hope. Make no mistake, all military spouses can thrive when they understand and accept the unique nature and challenges of military life.

My Experience

In the past, I personally reserved the acclaimed title of *thriving* for times when everything was "perfect." I told myself I had to be in the best shape or training to compete at a new physical level. I had to challenge myself mentally by obtaining higher education or working toward a promotion. I should be emotionally strong and stable. I needed close friends and to be an active volunteer in our church. Pretty unrealistic. I put a ridiculous amount of demands on myself and ended up missing the small moments to celebrate when I was thriving. In trying to reach perfection in so many areas, I actually ended up more unbalanced.

My emotional well-being typically took the hit, as it was easier to hide. Outwardly, you can look put together while you're a mess inside. I recall my second year in Montana in 2005. My husband and I were stationed at two different bases while we were both still active duty. I filled up my weeks with graduate classes, dual internships, instructing spin classes, and running the youth program at our church. I even had Friday deployed date nights with my girlfriend where we would scour the recent Cooking Light Magazine to make elaborate dinners for each other. My husband was going through an intense year of training for Special Ops and was probably just as busy. Most would think we were thriving, yet the intensity and separation were taking a toll on our emotional well-being and marriage.

In December, after six months apart, I drove to Bozeman to pick him up. As we pulled into our driveway, he was appalled to see three feet of snow and ice packed onto our drive. You see, I have a tendency to be a little passive-aggressive (think eye-rolling, banging pots and pans a little louder, and witty sarcasm, to name a few). My epic display had to be this—when I decided NOT to shovel for four months in Montana, in the winter, in negative seventy-degree weather because, well, I was angry I had to do it all myself. He spent four hours chiseling away the ice, which prompted a Come to Jesus conversation about how we were "really" doing.

The struggles of that year were often met with comments of, "This is what you both chose to do." (Something we end up hearing a lot as military spouses.) So it came as a surprise to many when we decided, during that Christmas break, that I would separate from the military the next year. We found ourselves on an unbalanced trajectory, moving at lightning speed. The little moments lacked joy because the big picture was so exhausting. We chose this significant change over permanent damage to our emotional and marital well-being.

I've learned that being "perfect" is unrealistic; being real is finding balance. It is an honest continual *reevaluation* of what is important to my family and me. I relish the small moments to celebrate. I praise my children when they are enjoying nature by climbing on their favorite Princess Rock and Falcon Rock in Colorado. I feel blessed when my husband and I can go on walks with our dog and share the highs and lows of our days. These small moments help me thrive, and when I add them all up, they help balance so many parts of my life.

So, how does one learn to thrive and not just survive? As my previously mentioned experience suggests, this is not always an easy feat. The field of positive psychology has coined the term "flourishing," in which researchers Corey Keyes and Jon Haidt detail a life lived with high levels of emotional, psychological, and social well-being. In essence, people whose life is flourishing have a passion for life, are engaged with others in their community, and bounce back from personal challenges.[1] One example at the collegiate level is what is referred to as the thriving quotient (TQ). Developed by professors who wanted to determine when students are thriving (instead of failing), it assesses engaged learning, academic determination, positive perspective, diverse citizenship, and social connectedness.[2]

Much like a professor's interest in their students, the military also wants to know how to better help families succeed. In 2015, the RAND Corporation conducted extensive research into five domains associated with military familial success: family belief systems, family organizational patterns, family support systems, family communication/ and problem-solving, and the physiological and psychological health of family members. Subsequently, a guide and associated programs were developed to better serve the needs of military families.[3]

> [Thriving] appears to come down to an individual
> experiencing a sense of development, of getting
> better at something, and succeeding at mastering
> something. In the simplest terms, what underpins it
> is feeling good about life.
> —Dr. Daniel Brown, 2017[4]

There are many ways to help yourself or others to thrive. I was introduced to one such tool in graduate school.

People of all ages recognize that a starfish has five distinct arms that work together gracefully. If an arm breaks off, the starfish can regrow it so it can continue to thrive in its environment. Your ability to thrive may be similar to a starfish. In other words, you might need to exchange some of your needs so that you can thrive. That is, while most people are able to thrive in some areas, they may neglect others. The following exercise is designed to remind you to balance these different areas.[5]

On a large sheet of paper, draw a starfish like the one shown below. Label each of the five arms with a thriving area: physical, mental, emotional, social, or spiritual. Consider how well you are meeting your needs in each area by describing how you are meeting each need. You can fill the space with people, activities, symbols, or words to portray how you are thriving. You may be surprised that some arms may be full while others are less so.

Now, let's take it one step further. Recalling the five dimensions mentioned above: physical, mental, emotional, social, or spiritual, assign a scale score of 1–10. (1 = an absence of thriving and 10 = the highest level.) Rate your current level to each of the areas you drew on your starfish. Finally, write down ideas on how you can grow to enhance your score in that area (if you think necessary).[5]

Thriving Assessment

Physical Thriving: My current level is a _____. I can move higher by ...

_____

_____

_____

_____

Mental Thriving: My current level is a _____. can move higher by ...

_____

_____

_____

_____

Emotional Thriving: My current level is a _____. I can move higher by ...

_____

_____

_____

_____

Social Thriving: My current level is a _____. I can move higher by ...

_____

_____

_____

_____

Spiritual Thriving: My current level is a _____. I can move higher by ...

_____

_____

_____

_____

Figure 21. Adapted from Echterling, Cowan, Evans, Staton, Viere, McKee, Presbury, and Stewart 2002. *Thriving: A Manual for Students in the Helping Professions.* New York: Houghton Mifflin Company.

When you have completed the above tasks, look to see if the five thriving areas are balanced. If not, what can you do to balance each of those areas? When you complete this exercise (and share your results with others), you will find that thriving looks very different to each of us.

Choosing Joy
Lindsey's Story

My mother-in-law once told me, "Wherever you put your focus is what you will become." I choose to put my focus on joy; I want to be known as a woman filled with joy. It is an everyday choice to wake up and choose joy over anything else. It doesn't mean I am always happy, but in my heart, I am content, thankful, blessed, and fulfilled. Some days the choice is easier to make than other days, but it is a choice. As the spouse of a military member, I feel like I have been given many different opportunities to test the theory of choosing joy.

For the first twenty-eight years of my life, I had it pretty darn amazing. I grew up in a military home with two loving parents and a fantastic sister. I earned a scholarship to attend the out-of-state school of my dreams, entered into the military myself, and eventually met and married Jeremy Fresques, the man of my dreams. A little over a year after getting married, Jeremy was killed in Iraq. My whole life was suddenly and unexpectedly flipped on its head. As painful as this experience was, I knew I didn't want to become the poor, depressing widow no one wanted to be around. I had known someone like that, and I didn't want to let myself become her. I chose to meet other widows who had been through it and also maintained a positive attitude. I leaned on my faith, attended conferences, joined grief groups, and did things (hello, sky diving!) my husband had wanted me to do. I used my situation to brief incoming wing and group commanders about notification procedures so hopefully other future widows and widowers would have the most dignified experience they could. Knowing I could help someone else made my situation have some purpose and, in effect, gave me healing. I didn't want the fact that I was a widow to define me. It is not who I am, but it is something that happened to me.

Almost two years later, I met my second husband. I knew right away there was something special about him. Not only did he love my dog, but also he didn't run away at the term "widow." I love his sense of humor and his love of service to others as well. There are still days when I look back and can start to feel sorry for myself for losing my first husband, but through choice, I choose to be thankful to have been married to two great men. My current husband's job has given me the opportunity to interact with all sorts of other spouses. When I was married to Jeremy, I didn't see the value of being involved as a spouse. When he died, I realized just how important military spouse-to-spouse relationships can be. There really is no one who can help you like someone who has been through it themselves. Those spouse-to-spouse relationships really helped me again when Scott and I tried to navigate the world of infertility. It was a lot easier to choose joy when I knew I wasn't the only one who was going through it. Our infertility journey ended better than we could have imagined when God placed our little girl into our arms through the gift of adoption. We would be amiss if we weren't willing to talk about infertility or adoption and pass along some hope to those who might be suffering through the same difficult situation.

When our daughter was about a year old, we were facing down our tenth military assignment. We were living in DC and *expected to stay there. Instead, we ended up with a short-notice assignment to Kuwait. Every assignment is stressful. There is the actual moving process, the goodbyes, the reinventing yourself when you arrive, making new friends, finding a new job or volunteer cause, and setting up your life at the new location. You can focus on the excitement of the new adventure, or you can focus on the stress. For my other nine moves, I was able to focus on the positive. This unexpected move to Kuwait, however, was really difficult for me. After the stress of the actual move was over, I found myself at home with a toddler in a country that was dirty, dangerous to drive in, and void of activities I would normally participate in. My normal coping skills include working out, getting involved in a church, eating healthily, spending time outside, traveling and seeing new things, and making at least one close friend as soon as I can after moving.*

In Kuwait, it took me over a year to get into any of my coping skills and find my groove. I should have chosen joy, but I chose to have a pity party instead. It made for a much longer two years than necessary. After meeting some new friends in the second year and the hope of a new assignment back to Okinawa, I had a whole new perspective again. I looked back and realized how much easier things would have been if I had chosen to focus on the positives instead of the things I didn't like.

After all these years and experiences, I am still surprised at how a good attitude can make a real difference. We arrived in Okinawa and had our household goods delivered, only to find out the moving company lost almost 2,000 pounds of our belongings. Unfortunately, the majority of our lost items were irreplaceable, sentimental items, including the flags from Jeremy's coffins, his beret and boots, and the last possessions of his I owned. The moving company lost our around 400 Christmas ornaments that were the love gifts my parents gave every year, representing all of our interests and travels. It was extremely difficult to focus on all of the missing items as we filed our claim. Instead of letting it drag me down, I chose to focus on the perspective. In the grand scheme of things, the missing items are just things. God taught me some good lessons about being attached to possessions.

It might be the life experiences I have gone through or watching others, but I have definitely found life to be much more enjoyable when you choose joy. Life will always give you plenty of opportunities to show you what you are made of. Difficult times are inevitable, but it is always a choice on how you respond.

—Lindsey Rowe, Air Force Spouse

Thriving can become a normal part of life. The fact is we can find contentment in ordinary experiences that add to our quality of life. Brené Brown writes, in *I Thought It Was Just Me*, "We seem to measure the value of people's contributions (and sometimes their entire lives) by their level of public recognition. In other words, worth is measured by fame or fortune. Our culture is quick to dismiss quiet, ordinary, hard-working men and women. In many instances, we equate ordinary with boring or, even more dangerously, ordinary has become synonymous with meaningless."[6]

Surviving to Thriving
Linda's Story

Phil, my husband of twenty-three years, was killed by someone he liked and trusted—someone he should have been able to trust because he wore a friendly uniform. Worse yet, the killer shot nine Americans in a room with over twenty other NATO Afghan troops, yet not one of them stood up or came to the defense of any of the men and one woman killed that day. In the immediate days after my husband had been assassinated, I couldn't get through five minutes without thinking of my devastating loss. This loss included more than the loss of my husband. It included the loss of faith in my country, my Air Force, my friendships, and myself. I fixated on the end and on the moments too awful to comprehend.

I could not sleep because of the intrusive thoughts that left me waking with tears and gasping for air. I isolated myself because I couldn't deal with the fear of figuring out life without Phil. I became a walking wounded woman who kept people at arm's length. I was afraid to feel. I consumed myself with work and with running. To the outside, I looked like I had it all together, but every waking moment and then in nighttime dreams, I was consumed with a yearning for what I did not have.

Two years after Phil had been killed, I was running the Boston Marathon when the first bomb hit. I was one stoplight from the finish line. I could see the finish line. The chaos didn't register until the second blast. I fled for my life. I found myself cowering under a table in a Dunkin Doughnuts shop. I couldn't tell you how I got there, but as I lay there, broken, something snapped. I could not let terrorism take any more from me. They already had taken my dreams for my future. Terrorism wasn't taking my running too.

I began to fight to thrive vs. survive. Instead of fleeing from my fears, I began to face them. My knees would shake; I would get physically sick, but each time, I accomplished even a small victory in standing up to my fear, I began to see possibilities where there were none before. It hasn't been easy, but I am living vs. surviving.

I made choices that many could not understand. I began running all over the world, and I took a job in first Germany and then Japan. I began to do public advocacy and to mentor other trauma survivors because it allowed something positive to come out of the worst moments of my life. Helping others became a way to honor and remember Phil, who lost his life far too soon.

I also fought to forgive Phil's assassin, not because it meant anything to him or to his country, but because it freed up my heart. I fight to forgive often, but the killer no longer has permanent real estate in my heart. Forgiveness isn't linear, and there are times I have to make a conscious effort to work through the anger and bitterness, even more than eight years later. On the days I am the angriest or the saddest, I look for people to do random acts of kindness to because it gets my internal focus off of myself and my feelings onto someone else who may be hurting also.

I liken the journey to thrive vs. survive to a marathon. I have run over 170 marathons. There is never one that I haven't wanted to quit. I know that I will feel worse tomorrow and the next day, but I also know that if I look at only the step ahead, I can get there. I may fall down. I may get lost. I may need a friend to encourage me, but I can run the race if I focus only on the step or moment in front of me.

Trauma is like that. In the immediate aftermath, a person survives one moment at a time. They cannot look too far ahead because it is too overwhelming to the crushed soul. At a point in the storm, a person will realize that the crushing moments are not coming at the same frequency. It is at that point a choice can be made—a choice to thrive vs. survive by looking for opportunities and meaning or changing the events and loss they have brought. While a person cannot change the events or the tragedies, they can choose the way forward. It is in that choice that a person becomes a better person than the person before.

—Linda Ambard, Air Force Spouse

The power to thrive is within all of us. As Lindsay and Linda's stories suggest, in spite of unavoidable setbacks, they made conscious choices to focus on thoughts (joy and thriving) that helped them maintain a more rational response to the situations they faced. While some setbacks are certainly more significant than others, focusing on the emotional choices has helped them to maintain a healthier response in spite of uncontrollable circumstances.

Rational Behavioral Technique 7
Rational Emotive Imagery (REI)

*My mind is full of terrible misfortunes—most
of which never happened.*
—Mark Twain

Imagination is a unique feature of being human. I love watching my children play, how they can transform blankets and pillows into pirate ships surrounded by molten lava. In other instances, they can imagine they are beautiful princesses (I have two girls) who, using the same blankets and pillows, miraculously transform a ship into a fairy tale castle. In that moment, they become these fictitious characters created solely in their minds.

Your imagination can work much the same way, as it can create a personal reality in which you think, feel, and act according to the mental script you have created. You have now completed your first rational self-analysis (RSA) and understand the rational way to think, feel, and behave. You also probably feel better about the situation you wrote about. However, you probably don't feel a great deal better while in the actual situation itself. Why do you think that is? Knowing how to think and act does not always mean you automatically feel better. Changing thoughts and behaviors are much easier than changing feelings.

Our next step is to change those unpleasant feelings by using your imagination. Imagining yourself in those old situations, but with rational thoughts and behaviors, can transform you into the "character" you wanted to be! It's going well beyond faking it until you make it. You have to think, feel, and act yourself into becoming the person you want to be. You have to make it real.

So, how exactly do you do this? The most effective way is with daily mental practice. That means every single day for the next week you are going to practice Rational Emotive Imagery (REI) by following these steps.[7]

Rational Emotive Imagery (REI) Steps

1. Prepare for REI:

- Complete a RSA from last chapter. (Pick an event you want to work on; look at your exercise from Chapter 6.)
- Read the rational side of the RSA.
- Do the Instant Behavior Feeling Maneuver (slow breathing): inhale and exhale deeply for five seconds and hold your breath/relax for three to four seconds. Repeat three to five times.

2. Do the REI:

- Vividly picture the event or situation you described.
- Picture yourself thinking, "I keep myself calm thinking …" and imagine you are thinking and believing the rational side of your self-analysis.
- Imagine feeling and acting the way you want to.
- Imagine yourself feeling and acting the way you wrote down you wanted to in your self-analysis.

3. If you begin to feel upset:

- Stop and relax. Clear your mind, take some deep breaths, and go back to REI.
- If you continue to feel upset, discontinue the REI. Try again another time.

4. When to do an REI:

- Try to pick four times a day when it is convenient to do it.
- Schedule time to do it.
- Try to pick a time when you are likely to do it. (In the morning when you wake up, after exercising, before bed, or on the way home from activities).

5. REI is NOT Pretending:

- You are doing this for yourself, not for others.
- You are following a successful procedure.
- You are working toward better emotional health

Figure 22. Adapted from Maultsby, M. C. and Hendricks, M.A. 1974. *You and Your Emotions*. Self-Help Books Divisions: Kentucky.

Recall the example RSA from Chapter 6 below. The REI concepts will follow this example to show you how it works.

RSA from Chapter 6

A. FACTS and EVENTS:	Da. CAMERA CHECK:
The military made a bad call (subject); they are making us move after eighteen months instead of the promised three years.	My husband's boss just called and informed him that we have to move to Florida in March.
B. SELF TALK:	**Db. CHALLENGE & ALTERNATIVES**
(B1) My husband's boss is an idiot.	(D1) He is an "idiot" in an untrue statement. It's not based on fact. (**R: not real**) It's an organization that can make quick decisions that are frustrating. (**S: it is not making me feel the way I want to feel.**) (**W: it did not protect my well-being.**)
(B2) They are playing favorites to other people in the squadron because I know they have granted assignment extensions.	(D2) I don't know that they are playing favorites and assuming this is only making me upset. (**R: not real**) (**S: not making me feel the way I want to feel.**) (**O: it is not helping me avoid conflict with others.**)
(B3) It's unfair; they never consider our family's needs and wants.	(D3) What's fair is not a relevant issue. (**O: it is not helping me avoid unwanted conflict with others**) What they did is not illegal. We have to move because it is what his job requires. (**D: it did not help achieve goals/destination**) (**S: it did not help me feel the way I want to**).
C1. FEELINGS:	**E1. DESIRED FEELINGS:**
Anger, hostility	Calm disappointment about not being able to stay in the current location.
C2. ACTIONS:	**E2. DESIRED ACTION**
Scream at my husband and work myself up over the pending move.	Do not scream at my husband. Calmly discuss the news with family or friends.

REI SCRIPT

1.	Find a comfortable place and relax your body. Inhale and exhale slowly for five minutes. Now picture the event that happened in your RSA. (For this example, it will be the unexpected PCS.)
2.	I am sitting at home with my husband after we have finished dinner. We are discussing what activities the kids have the rest of the week and what we are going to do over the weekend. We are enjoying our evening together.
3.	My husband's cell phone vibrates, and he immediately picks it up and tells me, "Give me a second; it's my boss." He leaves the room to take the phone call. I remain calm thinking that everything will be OK and there is no need to worry about what the phone call is about. My husband returns to tell me, "SMSgt Jones just told me we have to move to Florida in the spring because a job opened up and I need to fill it."
4.	I keep myself calm thinking, "The military is full of unexpected situations, but I know we can handle it. The decisions they make are out of my control, but by being calm and rational right now, I'll be able to handle this better for my family. I am disappointed by the news, but I know my husband's job is important to our family."
5.	Therefore, I calmly look at my husband and say, "I am disappointed we have to move so quickly, but I understand this happens. Please be patient with me, as it is going to take some time for me to accept this. Are you willing to help me tell the kids and our family, as I know they will be disappointed too?"'

Table 9. Lowe, K. 2019. "REI Script: Military Spouse Application." Thrive On, LLC.

Practicing REI is the fastest way to improve the way you think, feel, and act. Your imagination can help you thrive on to new possibilities!

While this may seem awkward at first, practicing this way of thinking will often allow it to feel more comfortable and natural.

Reflection Questions

(1) Describe a time in which your military family was/is thriving.

_____

_____

_____

_____

_____

_____

_____

(2) What areas do you find you thrive in the most? (Recall the five areas: physical, mental, emotional, social, or spiritual.) Why?

_____

_____

_____

_____

_____

_____

_____

(3) What do you think you can do to help other military spouses thrive?

_____

_____

_____

_____

_____

_____

_____

_____

(4) Write down one thriving goal you want to obtain in the next year as a military spouse/military family.

_____

_____

_____

_____

_____

_____

_____

_____

_____

_____

(5) List out four smaller bite-sized (quarterly) goals that will help you obtain your overall goal.

Exercises

(1) Conduct the starfish analogy of the five areas of thriving, and write down the pictures/words/thoughts that describe each area for YOU.[5]

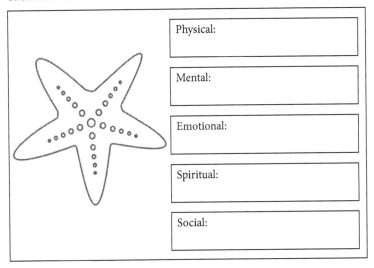

Physical:

Mental:

Emotional:

Spiritual:

Social:

(2) Practice REI at least once a day for the next week. Use the following steps (on the following page), and write down your reflections after each time you conduct the REI.[7]

1. Prepare for REI:

- Complete a RSA from last chapter. (Pick an event you want to work on; look at your exercise from Chapter 6.)
- Read the rational side of the RSA.
- Do the Instant Behavior Feeling Maneuver (slow breathing): inhale and exhale deeply for five seconds and hold your breath/relax for three to four seconds. Repeat three to five times.

2. Do the REI:

- Vividly picture the event or situation you described.
- Picture yourself thinking, "I keep myself calm thinking …" and imagine you are thinking and believing the rational side of your self-analysis.
- Imagine feeling and acting the way you want to.
- Imagine yourself feeling and acting the way you wrote down you wanted to in your self-analysis.

3. If you begin to feel upset:

- Stop and relax. Clear your mind, take some deep breaths, and go back to REI.
- If you continue to feel upset, discontinue the REI. Try again another time.

4. When to do an REI:

- Try to pick four times a day when it is convenient to do it.
- Schedule time to do it.
- Try to pick a time when you are likely to do it. (In the morning when you wake up, after exercising, before bed, or on the way home from activities).

5. REI is NOT Pretending:
- You are doing this for yourself, not for others.
- You are following a successful procedure.
- You are working toward better emotional health

Day 1: Write down your reactions after completing the REI.

_____

_____

_____

_____

_____

_____

Day 2: Write down your reactions after completing the REI.

_____

_____

_____

_____

_____

_____

Day 3: Write down your reactions after completing the REI.

_____

_____

_____

_____

_____

Day 4: Write down your reactions after completing the REI.

_____

_____

_____

_____

_____

_____

Day 5: Write down your reactions after completing the REI.

_____

_____

_____

_____

_____

Day 6: Write down your reactions after completing the REI.

_____

_____

_____

_____

_____

Day 7: REVIEW!

_____

_____

_____

_____

_____

_____

_____

Sources

1. Keyes, C. L. M., and Haidt, J. (Eds.). 2003. *Flourishing: Positive Psychology and the Life Well-Lived.* Washington, DC: American Psychological Association.

2. Schreiner, L. A. 2010. "The Thriving Quotient: A New Vision for Student Success." About Campus, 15(2), 2–10.

3. Meadows, S. O., Sarah O. Meadows, Megan K. Beckett, Kirby Bowling, Daniela Golinelli, Michael P. Fisher, Laurie T. Martin, Lisa S. Meredith, Karen Chan Osilla. 2015. Family Resiliency in the Military. RAND, Corporation.

4. Sandoiu, A. 2017. "Psychologist Finds the Key to Thriving." Retrieved from https://www.medicalnewstoday.com/articles/319358.php.

5. Echterling, Cowan, Evans, Staton, Viere, McKee, Presbury, and Stewart. 2002. *Thriving: A Manual for Students in the Helping Professions.* New York: Houghton Mifflin Company.

6. Brown, B. 2007. *I Thought it Was Just Me (But it Isn't): Making the Journey from 'What Will People Think' to 'I am Enough.'"* Gotham Books: New York.

7. Maultsby, M. C. and Hendricks, M.A. 1974. *You and Your Emotions.* Self-Help Books Divisions: Kentucky.

8

Final Thoughts
Go Do Epic Things

May the road rise up to greet you and the wind be always at your back.
—Irish Blessing

How to **COPE** with your **ReSet**

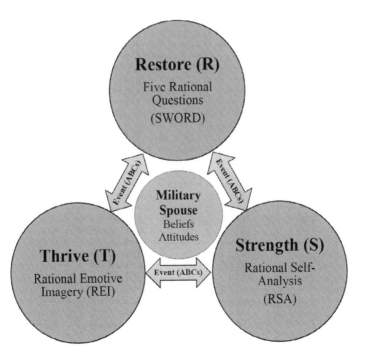

- **Restore (R)**
  Five Rational Questions (SWORD)
- **Military Spouse** Beliefs Attitudes
- **Strength (S)**
  Rational Self-Analysis (RSA)
- **Thrive (T)**
  Rational Emotive Imagery (REI)
- Event (ABCs)

My Experience

I've felt some of my highest highs and lowest lows as a military spouse, and if I had to give up one for the other, I would not. Those prideful moments where I have watched my husband declare his service to our nation would not be possible without the gut-wrenching fear of what his job entails. The courageous day my child taught her class about the "strength of a military community when my Daddy deploys" would never have occurred had she not sobbed herself to sleep embracing her "Daddy doll" for weeks on end. The collective triumph of completing this book would never have happened without the brave, honest, and raw stories of my fellow military spouses.

Yes, I've ridden out the lows by clinging to the highs, but man, how I wish some of the lows weren't quite so low. I have found that the lower you go, the harder it is to climb out. I have personally cycled through the military spouse life cycle so many times I've lost count, and I know I have several more cycles yet to come. But as each cycle approaches, I am more deliberate about my time to restore, to say I am not OK. I am more deliberate about strengthening the tools I have or reaching out for new ones. I am more deliberate about celebrating moments when my family is thriving.

Such deliberate choices were extremely important even as recently as this summer in 2019. Every summer has become an emotional trigger for me. I am either having to tear myself away from family and friends or helplessly watching while my children attempt to do the same. I had anticipated that this summer would be even more stressful because my children would be losing the only home they really knew. They would be experiencing culture shock integrating back into the United States, as this was a foreign land to them. Having Japanese women rub their blonde heads for good luck, teenage girls taking selfies with them,

Ramen noodles, shoeless restaurants, and a quiet, respectful society, this had become their "normal." Japan, to them, was home.

Thirty days out, I allowed myself all the "feels" as I said goodbye to people I loved, a job that was rewarding, and a squadron that had become family. I felt like I moderately had it under control until, well, I didn't. I tried my old coping skills, but at this point in time, in this specific situation, they just weren't enough. And I told myself that was OK. I reached out to a new MFLC to help guide me through the last thirty days in Japan, and I am so grateful for her. She made me see things a little more clearly, and she made me accountable—to myself and to my family. She challenged me to start journaling again, and this should come as no surprise: I love a good challenge. So I started to write, and just look at what it has become.

Ultimately, I know I will always look back at my time as a military spouse with pride and joy because these moments have helped defined who and I am and who I am yet to become.

Revisiting Where You Are At

You have diligently worked through this book for approximately seven weeks, and although change does not come quickly, positive change can happen given persistent practice. In order to see your progress, let's revisit two of the rating scales.

Fordyce Emotions Questionnaire

In general, how happy or unhappy do you usually feel? Check the ONE statement below that best describes your average happiness.[1]

_____ 10. Extremely happy (feeling ecstatic, joyous, fantastic)

_____ 9. Very happy (feeling really good, elated)

_____ 8. Pretty happy (spirits high, feeling good)

_____ 7. Mildly happy (feeling fairly good and somewhat cheerful)

_____ 6. Slightly happy (just a bit above normal)

_____ 5. Neutral (not particularly happy or unhappy)

_____ 4. Slightly unhappy (just a bit below neutral)

_____ 3. Mildly unhappy (just a bit low)

_____ 2. Pretty unhappy (somewhat "blue," spirits down)

_____ 1. Very unhappy (depressed, spirits very low)

_____ 0. Extremely unhappy (utterly depressed, completely down)

What percentage of the time do you feel happy, unhappy, or neutral? (Write down your percentages to add up to 100 percent below.)[2]

On average:

The percent of the time I feel happy is _____ percent.
The percent of the time I feel unhappy is _____ percent.
The percent of the time I feel neutral is _____ percent.

Authentic Happiness Scale

Below are five statements that you may agree or disagree with. Using the 1–7 scale below, indicate your agreement with each item by placing the appropriate number on the line preceding that item.

7 = Strongly agree
6 = Agree
5 = Slightly agree
4 = Neither agree nor disagree
3 = Slightly disagree
2 = Disagree
1 = Strongly disagree

___ In most ways, my life is close to ideal.
___ The conditions of my life are excellent.
___ I am completely satisfied with my life.
___ So far, I have gotten the important things I want in my life.
___ If I could live my life over, I would change nothing.

___ Total

30–35 Extremely satisfied, much above average
25–29 Very satisfied, above average
20–24 Somewhat satisfied, average for American adults
15–19 Slightly dissatisfied, a bit below average
10–14 Dissatisfied, clearly below average
5–9 Very dissatisfied, much below average[3]

What are your current scores? (Write them below.) How did your current scores compare to previous Fordyce Emotions Questionnaire and Authentic Happiness Scale scores recorded in Chapters 1 and 4, respectively? Did they go up, down, or remain the same? Why do you think your score did or did not change?

Fordyce Emotions Questionnaire (Ch. 1)	Authentic Happiness Scale (Ch. 4)
First Score:	First Score:
Current Score:	Current Score:
What change did you notice and why?	What change did you notice and why?

By using these tools whenever you enter a new stage of life, you can measure how you react to change, both socially and emotionally. Tools such as these can be utilized even after you are no longer a military spouse—well, at least an active duty spouse!

Retirement/Separation

While no one remains an active duty spouse forever, the service-related experiences will forever be part of who we are. This time is but ONE chapter in your life, and you should be immensely proud of what you have accomplished and overcome. However, the challenges of life do not end once the active duty member retires, but rather they morph into different types of challenges. As such, I encourage you to start thinking about this transition and how the techniques discussed in this book can help you to emotionally prepare for life's challenges outside of the military.

The 1 Percent Who Serve
Marybeth's Story

About 1 percent of today's population serves in the US military. That leaves about 99 percent of the population who have not served. Given this statistic, we find that military personnel are uniquely different from the general population.

After twenty-six years in the military, my husband retired. No parade, no big party (believe me, I sat through hundreds), just a small group get together near his office in the Pentagon with sandwiches and soft drinks. How did I feel? At the time, I was elated! Finally, no one would have his ear 24/7. We could have choices: where to live and where to vacation (yes, vacation), and no one owned us.

Two weeks later, my husband started a new job in an unfamiliar city. Once again, our household goods were loaded onto a truck (for the fourteenth time). We had to leave our new college graduate in Virginia. We kissed our youngest son goodbye at the Air Force Academy and prayed that our oldest, a lieutenant in the Air Force, would be safe in South Korea. Why does this still feel the same?

What I found difficult about our new life was most of the population has no clue what my life as a military spouse had been like. We moved two more times as a result of my husband's second career. I taught school at two of the locations, cared for one aging parent, and buried three others. Indeed, the only constant was the American Flag flying outside our home.

It wasn't until my husband retired from his second career that I realized why I was able to endure all the transitions we had experienced. I had learned to look at situations as positively as I could. As parents, our children are always of the utmost importance. As spouses, we have peaks and valleys in our lives, ups and downs we endure with the help of others. My go-to is God and prayer. He never lets me down and has helped me through lots of messy situations.

I have two wonderful and strong military spouse daughters-in-law, one of whom is the author of this book. They both have had much harder military experiences than I perhaps, due to the never-ending conflicts around the world or because of their very high expectations for themselves. I can tell you I am very proud of all the military and their families. They may be only 1 percent of the population, but I thank God every day for that 1 percent!

—Marybeth Lowe, Air Force Spouse

As so eloquently noted above, recently separated or retired military families need to be emotionally prepared for life's transitions. Many families serve in the military for twenty years or more but are unprepared for the transition to civilian life without the financial and social support they previously experienced. In 2018, the Military Family Lifestyle Survey highlighted this fact. Thirty-seven percent of veteran respondents shared that there is a need for a stronger support network to help a military family's transition to civilian life. While transition programs are available to those exiting the military, only 65 percent of veterans take advantage of such support and 50 percent of those report the program does not adequately prepare them for a successful transition.[4] Once discharged, the active-duty member becomes a veteran and no longer part of the active-duty community. This is a significant transition where the veterans can experience symptoms of grief associated with their perceived loss of military self.[5] Such grief and subsequent stress during the transition from military to civilian life have been associated with mental and physical health problems. [6] Knowing and using the tools shared in this book cannot only help you transition but also enable you to help your spouse navigate their new identity.

It is common for military families (retired or separated) to have difficulty finding a new home, locating a job, and integrating into civilian communities. The Military Family Lifestyle Survey reported that 47 percent of veteran military spouses indicated transitioning to civilian life was "difficult" or "very difficult."[4] In many ways, transitioning into civilian life may be even more stressful for military families than reflected by current research.

Rational Behavioral Technique 8
Honest Practice

Man is the inventor of his own happiness.
—Thoreau

Behavioral change always seems difficult at first. I remember having to change my wake-up time to four a.m. when I started a new job. Every morning. I wanted to roll over, hit snooze, and wake up at a more reasonable hour. I can't say that I was ever ecstatic about waking up at four in the morning, but after several weeks, it became a little easier. This is true for any new behavior. At first it seems difficult, but the more you practice it, the easier it becomes. The goal is to reeducate yourself to act in a different way. Like all learning, you need to practice, practice, practice (and offer yourself a little grace along the way)!

You have come such a long way since the beginning of the book! In fact, look at all you have learned as part of your Emotional Reeducation.

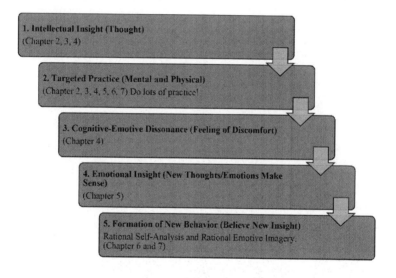

1. Intellectual Insight (Thought)
(Chapter 2, 3, 4)

2. Targeted Practice (Mental and Physical)
(Chapter 2, 3, 4, 5, 6, 7) Do lots of practice!

3. Cognitive-Emotive Dissonance (Feeling of Discomfort)
(Chapter 4)

4. Emotional Insight (New Thoughts/Emotions Make Sense)
(Chapter 5)

5. Formation of New Behavior (Believe New Insight)
Rational Self-Analysis and Rational Emotive Imagery.
(Chapter 6 and 7)

You have the tools, but if you REALLY want to change, and I mean really change, you need to practice these techniques intentionally and with honesty, not pretending to do so. Are you pretending? Or are you really trying to change? If you are unsure, then take a look on the next page.

Honest vs. Pretend Practice

Honest Practice	Pretend Practice
1. Act as if you already know the behavior you want.	1. Act as if you already know the behavior you DON'T want, with little intention to change.
2. Replaced old beliefs with new ones that are rational for your new behavior.	2. Maintained your old beliefs, yet tried to get new behavioral results.
3. Sincerely intend to make practiced behavior your NEW trait.	3. Do not intend to make a new behavior a personality trait or haven't decided yet.
4. Use new rational thinking and behaviors that produce new behaviors.	4. Refuse to use proven effective thinking and behaviors that produce new behaviors.
5. Primarily interested in how your new behavior affects yourself.	5. Primarily interested in how your new behavior affects someone else.
6. Show more and more evidence that genuine learning is taking place.	6. Do not show more and more evidence that learning is taking place.

Table 10. Adapted from Maultsby, M. C. and Hendricks, M.A. 1974. *You and Your Emotions*. Self-Help Books Divisions: Kentucky.

After reading these characteristics, you should have insight into whether you believe you are being honest with yourself. The question is whether you are improving your emotional well-being or just pretending?

Final Steps in Developing the Emotional and Behavioral Habits You Want

To determine what stage you are in as part of your Emotional Reeducation, check the items on the next page. This brief survey should help you gauge your current state of social-emotional well-being and where you possibly have yet to go.[7]

Emotional Reeducation Checklist

Step	Definition	Check If You Have Completed
Dissatisfaction	I am dissatisfied by a present habit (thought, emotion, behavior, or feeling).	
Learn	I have learned effective ways to change habits.	
Decide	I have decided and stated, "I want to change _____, and this is how I will do it."	
Commitment	I have made a strong commitment. "I'm going to change _____. I'm going to do all that is necessary and not stop until I reach my goal."	
Think	I am thinking about my new positive thoughts, consistently.	
Behave	I am acting the way I want to, and it fits new thoughts, consistently.	
Ignore	I have felt uncomfortable at times, but I am ignoring those feelings because I know they come with new habits.	
Emotional Insight	I have gained new emotional insight!	
New Habit	I have developed a new habit!	
New Lifestyle	I am starting to see a change in my life due to my new habit!	

Table 11. Adapted from Maultsby, M. C. and Hendricks, M.A. 1974. *You and Your Emotions*. Self-Help Books Divisions: Kentucky.

Being a rational thinker and "doer" will help you no matter what stage of life you are in. As a military spouse, learning how to think, feel, and act rationally will continue to serve you long after your military tenure is over. Make no mistake, this is not meant to be a keto, paleo, Adkins, or fasting diet. However, like eating better and becoming more active contributes to a healthier body, the skills you've gained through this book will result in a new emotionally healthy way of life for your entire family and you.

The Military Family

Active Duty Member

Three hundred twenty-one is another significant number. It is the number of active-duty members who committed suicide in 2018, and the highest rate recorded since tracking began in 2001.[8] In August 2019, the chief of staff of the Air Force, General Goldfein, officially called for a "tactical pause" to address this issue. At that point, seventy-eight airmen had taken their lives, thirty more than the previous year.[9] Such is the concern over mental health issues associated with active duty service. Active duty members are required to endure significant stress, as reflected by CMSgt Nathan Cox.

Do Not Expect a Life Free From Suffering
Nathan's Story

Military members are called upon to perform and behave within two diametrically opposed environments—this tension is the key stressor for military members. The first environment is the home front, where emotional openness and familial/nurturing behavior are required. The second is the war front, where emotional hardness and ruthless performance are required. The challenge with understanding these two "fronts" is that only those who have truly experienced it understand, as Ziad Abdelnour aptly describes, "To those who understand, no explanation is necessary, to those who do not understand, no explanation is possible." Honestly, it is not important for the spouse to understand the war front, it is only important she understands the stress in navigating between the two and how these stressors may manifest.

Unfortunately, the military has not adequately equipped its members with the cognitive or behavioral tools to navigate the transitions between fronts. It is also unfortunate that the family typically bears the brunt of this oversight. The following are recommendations to the military spouse from someone who has lived on both fronts and has learned some lessons the hard way.

(1) *If your spouse does not or will not share their war experiences with you, do not take it personally. Sometimes they are lost in their head, reliving particularly nasty experiences, and the last thing they want to do is give it more power by giving voice to it (right or wrong). Additionally, they may not share because they simply do not want to lay the burden of those experiences on you; it is theirs to carry, not yours. Silence can be a gift.*

(2) *As alluded to earlier, your spouse may not know how to "turn off" and is struggling with the transition between warrior and husband. Give them space, and*

recognize they are relearning to some extent what it means to be a daddy and husband. The attributes that make a great warrior typically make a terrible spouse, and the instincts that have been honed over months of combat are not so easily set aside. Coax them back into the family. They want to be there but carry baggage that was not there before and are trying to figure out how to fit it all in.

(3) *Accept that change is inevitable. The nature of your relationship will (and should) change as each of you change, based on your experiences. It is important to remember that the military member may have experienced significant events during their service that will have an impact on them. Do not hold overly tightly to the past, but embrace the present and accept your relationship as it is now. Simply because someone may experience trauma in their life, it does not mean that experience needs to be traumatic or even detrimental. It just means you have experienced life and now have a choice. You either cower down and let those experiences bury you or climb atop them and gain strength and perspective. The same holds true for the military family as you face tribulations and hardships together. The secret is this: do not expect a life free of suffering, but rather choose to overcome the suffering—together.*

—CMSgt Nathan Cox, Air Force

The Military Child

Military children have to endure moving approximately every 2.9 years.[10] Such frequent change can result in significant social and emotional stress, as well as educational challenges.[11] An alarming 1.7 million military children will move during any given school year, which is 2.4 times greater than their civilian counterparts.[12] As depicted by Brianna, we require our children to persevere after multiple moves in a similar fashion to that of their nonmilitary parent.

Never Give Up!
Brianna's Story

Hello, I'm Brianna, and I'm nine years old. I am a military child. Being a military child is not too easy. There are some challenges, but there are some fun things too. The biggest challenge is moving. It is hard because you have to say goodbye to your home, your friends, and your teacher. For example, when I had to move to Okinawa, I had to leave my friend Grace. When I moved to Okinawa, I felt sad that I left the people I know the most. I also was unhappy that I had to leave my grandparents.

I was not too sad, though, because there are also fun things about being a military child. For example, you get to explore new cultures and make new friends. I knew I would make new friends easily because probably everyone else would be trying to find a friend too! I was right! I did make great new friends! The other challenging part of being a military child is when your friends leave. Mine did—but I made new friends.

Part of being a military child is having to be responsible— like when my dad goes on trips for work, I have to step up to help my mom. It is not always easy being a military child, but I

keep going and never give up! The thing I always remember that my dad told me is to be strong and never give up! I always listen to my dad! Overall, I love being a military child!
　　　　　　　　　　　　　　　—Brianna, Military Child

Rest assured your military child is watching and learning from you. They want to understand how to tackle this challenging life you have chosen for them. But you can also learn from them—just look at Brianna's choices to look for the positive within the constantly changing style of her life. With proper support, all military children can navigate the social and emotional stress associated with military life. Modeling behavior is one of the most effective ways for children to learn. If you consistently model rational thoughts and behaviors, then your children (and maybe even your spouse!) are more likely to do the same.

The simple fact is, as the spouse of a member of the US Military, your family needs you, your spouse needs you, and the military needs you. Your service to our nation is heroic but comes at a cost. Do not let the price be your family, your self-worth, or your general well-being. Understand the unique nature of military life, anticipate and persevere in the face of social-emotional setbacks, practice effective coping strategies, and learn to thrive on to new possibilities.

Life challenges us all to make deliberate choices every day, not the least of which is the power to choose who you are and who you will become.

We Are Strong—We Are Vulnerable—We Are Capable— We Are Military Spouses

THRIVE ON

Reflection Questions

(1) How do you feel now that you have worked through the entire military spouse life cycle?

_____

_____

_____

_____

_____

_____

_____

(2) What stage do you relate most with? Why?

_____

_____

_____

_____

_____

_____

_____

_____

(3) Have you and your spouse discussed retirement/separation from the military? How do you feel about it?

_____

_____

_____

_____

_____

_____

_____

(4) Do you believe your spouse (active duty member) experiences stress? What signs and symptoms do you see? Have you discussed it with him or her? If not, do it today.

_____

_____

_____

_____

_____

_____

_____

_____

Exercises

(1) Check and see if you are being honest with yourself. Circle which side applies to you for each criteria.[7]

Honest Practice	Pretend Practice
1. Act as if you already know the behaviors you want.	1. Act as if you already know the behavior you DON'T want (little intention to change).
2. Replaced old beliefs with new ones that are rational for your new, desired behaviors.	2. Maintained your old beliefs, yet trying to get new behavior results.
3. Sincerely intend to make the practiced behaviors your NEW traits.	3. Do not intend to make a new behavior a personality trait or haven't decided yet.
4. Use new rational thinking and behaviors that produce new habitual behaviors.	4. Refuse to use proven effective thinking and behaviors that produce new behaviors.
5. Primarily interested in how your new behaviors affect yourself.	5. Primarily interested in how your new behavior affects someone else.
6. Show more and more evidence that genuine learning is taking place.	6. Do not show more and more evidence that learning is taking place.

(2) Check the steps you have completed. Then, make a plan for those you have not yet completed.

Step	Definition	Check if you have completed
Dissatisfaction	I am dissatisfied by a present habit (thought, emotion, behavior, and feeling).	
Learn	I have learned effective ways to change habits.	
Decide	I have decided and stated, "I want to change _____, and this is how I will do it."	
Commitment	I have made a strong commitment. "I'm going to change _____. I'm going to do all that is necessary and not stop until I reach my goal."	
Think	I am thinking about my new positive thoughts, consistently.	
Behave	I am acting the way I want to and it fits new thoughts, consistently.	
Ignore	I have felt uncomfortable at times, but I am ignoring those feelings because I know they come with new habits.	
Emotion Insight	I have gained new emotional insight!	
New Habit	I have developed a new habit!	
New Lifestyle	I am starting to see a change in my life from my new habit!	

Plan for those not completed and an anticipated completion date.

Step	Plan	Goal Date
Dissatisfaction		
Learn		
Decide		
Commitment		
Think		
Behave		
Ignore		
Emotion Insight		
New Habit		
New Lifestyle		

(3) Pass on what you have learned to others. Encourage other military spouses to start this study today!

Sources

1. Fordyce, Michael W. 1988. "A Review of Research on the Happiness Measures: A Sixty Second Index of Happiness and Mental Health." SpringerLink. Kluwer Academic Publishers.

2. Seligman, M. E. 2002. *Authentic Happiness: Using the New Positive Psychology to Realize Your Potential for Lasting Fulfillment.* New York: The Free Press.

3. Seligman, M. E. 2002. *Authentic Happiness: Using the New Positive Psychology to Realize Your Potential for Lasting Fulfillment.* New York: The Free Press.

4. Sonethavilay, H., Maury, R.V., Jurwitz, J. L., Uveges, R.L., Akin, J. L., Coster, J. L., and Strong, J.D. 2018. 2018 *Military Family Lifestyle Survey: Findings and Analysis.* Washington D.C.: Blue Star Families Department of Research and Policy.

5. Mobbs, M. C., and Bonanno, G.A. 2018. "Beyond War and PTSD: The Crucial Role of Transition Stress in the Lives of Military Veterans." *Clinical Psychology Review,* 59, 137–144.

6. Interian, A., Kline, A., Janal, M., Glynn, S., and Losonczy, M. 2014. "Multiple Deployments and Combat Trauma: Do Home Front Stressors Increase the Risk for Post-traumatic Stress Symptoms?" *Journal of Traumatic Stress,* 27(1), 90–97.

7. Maultsby, M. C. and Hendricks, M.A. 1974. *You and Your Emotions.* Self-Help Books Divisions: Kentucky.

8. Kime, P. 2019. "Active-Duty Military Suicide Rates at Record High in 2018." *Military.com.* Retrieved from http://download. militaryonesource.mil/12038/MOS/Reports/2016-Demographics-Report.pdf.

9. Pawlyk, O. 2019. "Air Force to Pause Operations After a Spike in Suicides." *Military.com.* Retrieved from https://www.military.com/daily-news/2019/08/01/air-force-pause-operations-after-spike-suicides.html.

10. Esqueda, M.C., Astor, R.A. and De Pedro, K. M. 2012. "A Call to Duty: Educational Policy and School Reform Addressing the Needs of Children from Military Families." *Educational Researcher*, 41, 61–70.

11. Millegan, J., McLay, R., and Engel, C. 2014. "The Effects of Geographic Moves on Mental Healthcare Utilization of Children." *Journal of Adolescent Health*, 55(2), 276–280.

12. Department of Defense. 2017. "Month of the Military Child." Retrieved from https://dod.defense.gov/News/Special-Reports/0417_militarychild/

Epilogue

The Military Spouse

刀

The Katana sword's symbol transmits strength, courage, and wisdom identical to our military spouses. The sword is made of unique material meticulously chosen for greatness. It is carefully strengthened with forged heat, bending, and molding to create its shape. It is painstakingly polished to demonstrate excellence. It is a survivor of decades of wounds and scars in battle, yet maintains strength from careful, deliberate restoration. The life of the Katana sword is accomplished, valued, and respected.

Military spouses have to endure constant stress. They are brave and strong. They are unique in their individual walks with little control over their paths, yet have a choice in the journey along the way. They are required to flex and bend in multiple environments that can leave deep emotional wounds. Yet remarkably, they continue to thrive because of their courageous choice to deliberately restore and strengthen over and over again. You, the military spouse, are accomplished, valued, and respected.

We Are Strong—We Are Vulnerable—We Are Capable—
We Are Military Spouses

About the Author

Dr. Kendra Lowe is a psychologist, author, and military spouse. As the founder and CEO of Thrive On, LLC she is committed to helping cultivate social and emotional health within military families.

Previously, she was a school psychologist for the Department of Defense, adjunct faculty for Central Texas College, columnist for *Military Spouse Magazine*, and an active duty airmen. She currently resides in Texas with her husband and three children.

Made in the USA
Columbia, SC
31 July 2020

14204523R00133